Dutch Gentlemen Adventurers
In Canada 1811 – 1893

DUTCH GENTLEMEN
ADVENTURERS
In Canada  1811–1893

Translated and Edited by

Jan Krijff &
Herman Ganzevoort

GRANVILLE ISLAND
PUBLISHING
www.granvilleislandpublishing.com

Library and Archives Canada Cataloguing in Publication

Dutch gentlemen adventurers in Canada, 1811–1893 / translated and edited by Jan Krijff & Herman Ganzevoort.

Includes translations of journals, articles, manuscripts, letters, and books.
Includes bibliographical references and index.
Issued in print and electronic formats.
ISBN 978-1-926991-32-0 (pbk.). — ISBN 978-1-926991-37-5 (ebook)

1. Travelers' writings, Dutch—Canada. 2. Travelers' writings, Dutch—Translations into English. 3. Dutch—Travel—Canada—History—19th century. 4. Canada—Description and travel. 5. Canada—Description and travel—Literary collections. 6. Canada—History—19th century—Anecdotes. I. Krijff, Jan Th. J., 1947-, translator, editor of compilation II. Ganzevoort, Herman, 1942-, translator, editor of compilation

FC72.D88 2013   917.104'03   C2013-906312-9
                                               C2013-906313-7

Editor: Kyle Hawke
Cover and text designer: Omar Gallegos

Granville Island Publishing Ltd.
212 – 1656 Duranleau St.
Vancouver, BC, Canada V6H 3S4

604-688-0320 / 1-877-688-0320
info@granvilleislandpublishing.com
www.granvilleislandpublishing.com

First published in March 2014
Printed in Canada on recycled paper

To Karen Lynn with love.
To Karen Green, with whom everything is possible.

Acknowledgements

The completion of the book was accomplished with the aid of a few in many various ways. Ted Bal brought his considerable expertise as a draftsman to creating the maps used in this book. Furthermore, we owe in particular a great debt of gratitude to Karen Green, who dedicated her time, energy and inspiration (in good times and bad) from the beginning to the completion of this project.

Contents

Reflections

When Jan Krijff came to me and suggested that we combine our forces to create a book of excerpts from the reminiscences of Dutch travellers in Canada in the 19th century, he introduced me to unique material which was virtually unknown in Canada and Holland. Due to the fact that my field of study and research had been Dutch emigration to Canada, primarily in the 20th century, I was unfamiliar with the travel literature that had preceded the emigration to North America. To my surprise, I met an entirely new group of Hollanders, distinctly different from those that had been the focus of my research and writing for over forty years.

Unlike most emigrants, who had elementary educations, were primarily of agricultural occupations and a working class social background, the travellers were educated, of high social class and whether of military background, scions of wealthy and influential families or young men preparing for public or governmental careers, their reports and reminiscences were read with interest. The writings helped shape the attitudes of many of their countrymen in regards to the unknown land which lay to the north of the United States of America.

Holland was familiar with the USA; it had supported the American Revolution and was the first foreign nation to recognize the republic. The United States soon became the focus of Dutch investment as the industrial and commercial revolution began to turn America in a new direction.

It was inevitable that as the Canadians began to build their railways and factories in the latter half of the century that

Dutch interest in possible investment possibilities grew apace. The completion of the Canadian Pacific Railway in 1885 was in no small way due to Dutch investment as was the growth of other industries.

Interest also grew in the land that the CPR had received as a government grant to cover its cost of construction. The Dutch came to view it as a possible answer to their shortage of land and surplus of agricultural workers. Canada offered cheap or free land, jobs and a social safety valve, just as the American frontier was closing.

When the gentlemen travellers made their social calls in Montreal it was to the movers and shakers of the new Canada. Their welcome as social equals was a recognition that the economic elite of the Netherlands would continue to play an important part in the development of Canada. Their reception was warm and welcoming.

It was the reports of the travellers and settlers that helped to change the perception of the Canadian West in Holland from a frozen wasteland or blazing desert to a limitless 'land of opportunity'. As the 19th century progressed, interest shifted from the touristic wonders of Niagara Falls to the Canadian West and the unexplored North. Canada now seemed to hold the promises that had formerly been the exclusive property of the USA and the Dutch gentlemen travellers left a legacy that was to play a pivotal role in the growth of this new nation.

Herman Ganzevoort
Calgary
December 2013

Preface

Some years ago, after one of my occasional excursions to second-hand bookstores, I emerged with a modest book about a Dutch sailor, Klaas Jacobs Kuipers, who had served on the high seas during the Napoleonic war. It was not until I later thumbed through the book at home that I noticed, to my surprise, the inclusion of a *petite histoire* about Kuipers' stay in Quebec City in 1811. This discovery led to the notion that there might be other writings by 19th-century Dutch travellers containing interesting commentaries about early Canada. The result of the search for relevant material was highly rewarding with the discovery of a wide diversity of other Dutch travel writings. It was also very gratifying to find that the commentators were savvy observers, who described their engagement with various people and provided a wealth of historical information and insight about early Canada. Wishing to make their stories available to an English-speaking audience, I approached my good friend Herman Ganzevoort about joining me in this endeavour. The narratives and passages are translated in English and in attempting to retain their authenticity, no corrections have taken place in any of the authors' observations. However, we did choose to place a few explanatory footnotes where we thought fit.

There are numerous studies regarding accounts of early travel in Canada. Anthologies of extracts from these have been published; some have been reprinted in their entirety. Most of the published travel stories came from British pens (and to a lesser extent from

American ones). Hence, most are from English-speaking travellers. In addition, there is a number of travel narratives in French.

This is the first collection of Dutch travel commentaries about Canada, which were crafted in the century when Canada became a nation and when she went through major advances in technical and economic development. The country as seen through Dutch eyes, provides yet another perspective on 19th-century Canada. Moreover, keeping these stories about Canada's history alive is also beneficial to understanding its culture, as, one would argue, is any study of history.

Jan Krijff

Introduction

Of the large variety of historical documents available, few provide the same connection with the people of the past as do personal writings, such as the ones presented in this book. It is because of the personal nature of these writings that it is, by no means, our intent to analyze, dissect and interpret all the views articulated about Canada by the writers of these journals. It is, of course, up to the reader to make his or her own observations and draw their own conclusions about what the writers had to say. That being said, we do want to share some background and contextual information.

Interest in Canada by the Dutch well precedes the 19th century; indeed it goes back about four hundred years. There have been Dutch footprints on Canadian soil since the 1600s. Amsterdam had grown explosively during the first half of the 17th century and became a trade centre of international importance. As an emerging commercial power, the Netherlands was exploring new markets in "het goutrijck Amerijcke" [gold-rich America], so-named by the prominent 17th century Dutch poet, Joost van den Vondel.[1] To secure and control their commercial interests, the Dutch established a colony on the north-eastern American shore with the village of New Amsterdam (later New York City) as its main hub. At that time, Dutch merchants living in close proximity to Fort Orange (later Albany) were engaged in the fur trade with the natives of New France, now Quebec. Meanwhile, Dutch shippers were seen on the eastern shores of Canada (Newfoundland), buying salted and dried codfish that they transported to and sold in the Mediterranean countries, the so-called "sack trade".[2]

In 1664, the Dutch colonial possessions in America were taken over by the English, cutting off direct Dutch influence over the continent. Dutch ships still continued to carry whalers to the Davis Strait and the waters off Labrador. Sailing to New France, however, was governed by Imperial law, which stated that only French ships were to sail between France and its colony New France. Despite these legal restrictions, well-equipped Dutch vessels with their respective crews were frequently chartered by French shipbrokers to make the journey to New France. With the English conquest of New France in 1760, all of Canada's territory became subject to the *British Navigation Acts* of 1651. Through this legislation, Oliver Cromwell intended that all trade to English colonies remained in the hands of British shippers. Consequentially, direct shipping between Holland and Canada came to a halt. Despite this specific trade restriction, savvy Dutch traders were still able to do business with Canada, for example through London, and also by exploiting alternate trade channels such as those through the Dutch West Indies and the United States. Dutch distillers, who for a large part operated for the export market, were still able to bring their product to the Canadian market. In 1810, an advertisement in *La Gazette de Quebec* showed that the firm Paterson, Grant & Co. in Quebec had Dutch Geneva (gin) for sale.[3] Drink also oozed into Montreal where, in 1821, the firm Macnider, Aird & Co. and later, in 1825, the firm Gillespie, Moffat & Co. informed the public of their 'Dutch Gin' in store.[4]

The measures imposed by the British government that had curtailed the free flow of goods, so essential to the prosperity of the Dutch economy, were soon regarded as water under the bridge in view of the political developments that came to pass at the end of the 18th century in America. Since the Netherlands was pre-eminently a trading nation, it was sympathetic to the stand taken by the Americans against its old enemy Great Britain. It foresaw a shift in the balance of power in Europe, which in turn would have worldwide political and trade-related repercussions. The Dutch financial community eagerly anticipated renewing trade relations and playing an important role in handling the banking requirements of an independent America. In 1782, Holland established official relations with the United States. The independence of the United States promoted not only a significant interest in the American political system but also a hunger for knowledge about all facets of American life. This land, being far away on the other side of the world, was then (and still is) a topic of intense interest. For the more progressive members of the Dutch establishment, the United States was seen as an experimental country, young and vast, with no history but with a future. In America, there were still things to be discovered. This was a territory to which a number of Dutch travellers came to satisfy their curiosity about the various peoples there and the untamed physical environment in which they lived.

In contrast, it seems, Canada did not have the same vibrant appeal. This may be because the country existed as a colony, within the folds of the cloak of the British Empire — *to wit*, British North America. It could also have been at play that information about Canada during the 19th century through newspaper articles and stories was never front-page news, at least not until the mid-1880s. However, Canada did get some coverage. For example, probably out of sympathy for their plight, the story of Irish emigrants to Canada was comprehensively covered in Dutch newspapers. Other notable matters reported were the Upper and Lower Canada rebellion of 1837–1838,[5] the large fire of June 28, 1845 in Quebec City,[6] the Fenian raids in 1866,[7] and in May 1883, the summons served upon Canada's prime minister, John A. Macdonald.[8]

The limited availability of information about Canada, compounded by a selective readership of newspapers in the Netherlands, could explain why Dutch emigrants bypassed Canada in large numbers in favour of the USA. Also the relatively small amount of trade between Holland and Canada rendered Canada less important to most large and influential Dutch merchant-houses. Hardly any Canadian products were to be seen by people in the Netherlands. On the other hand, the bold and shrewd distillers from Schiedam sold large quantities of Dutch gin during the last half of the 19th century, satisfying (or perhaps stimulating) the great Canadian thirst for hard liquor.[9] In order to enhance trade with Canada, the Dutch government was persuaded by the commercial establishment to facilitate trade by entering into official relations with Canada. It appointed the wealthy businessman Benjamin Homer-Dixon, born in the Netherlands, then living in Toronto, as the first Dutch Consul-General in the British North American colonies, in 1862.[10]

It was not until the last two decades of the century, during the International Colonial and Export Trade Exhibition in Amsterdam in 1883, that the Dutch public at large would be able to more easily obtain knowledge and information about Canada.[11] At the Exhibition, Canada was presented as *den Korentuin der Wereld* ('the world's grain garden'), particularly putting its hardy grains and seeds on display. To entice immigrants, exhibition advertisements touted that the average wages in Canada during 1881 and 1882, for bricklayers and road workers, plasterers, carpenters, and blacksmiths, were seven-and-a-half to ten florins per day.[12] This international multicultural exhibition also created an opportunity for the CPR to promote Canada in Holland as well as to the rest of the European continent.

In the meantime, by December of 1882, forty Amsterdam firms were highly interested in Canada, having decided to invest four million dollars in the CPR. The total Dutch interest in the CPR would rise to eight million dollars by 1885.[13] Clearly for their own benefit, these Dutch investors in both the CPR and their Canadian land holdings (along with the Canadian govern-ment and the Canadian Pacific Railway company itself) seized this opportunity to participate in the exhibition. The result was a display designed to glamorize Canada by portraying it as a civilized country full of richness and rapid development with unlimited possibilities for Dutch settlers and travellers in Western Canada.

Apart from the exhibition, Canada had a surprising trump card to play in its promotion efforts. During this period in time, the city of Amsterdam already had a diverse and reputable music scene. Amsterdam was also where Canada's own cultural scene was spotlighted, through its glamorous, international opera star and leading soprano, Emma Albani. She had first performed for and impressed the influential members of Dutch society during her appearance in Amsterdam on February 15, 1881. In March of 1884, she again delighted audiences in Amsterdam. These sophisticated and critical crowds, in all probability including some wealthy CPR shareowners, were in such rhapsody upon hearing her marvellous voice, that she was invited to return. Miss Albani responded favourably to this request and would travel four more times to the Netherlands to give memorable performances, her last in Amsterdam on March 3, 1891.[14]

Advertisement for Emma Albani's first concert in the Netherlands, 1881

Emma Albani

Publicity for Canada did not stop here. To further raise its growing acclaim, the CPR had entered the International Agriculture Exhibition also held in 1884 in Amsterdam, where it received a gold medal for its exhibit showing products grown on black clay ground without fertilizer along the CPR line.[15] Two years later, the CPR again drew notice, this time at the Bakery Exhibition held at the illustrious *Paleis voor Volksvlijt* ['Palace for the People'] in Amsterdam where it received gold and silver in the category 'milling'.[16] Eventually, the company opened a permanent exhibition at the office of René R. H. toe Laer, its representative in Amsterdam showing, in particular, products of Manitoba and the North West of Canada. On the walls were photographs, among them one depicting the dining hall at the Winnipeg station and one showing CPR railway carriages. The latter, according to the newspaper, make "travelling easy and makes one almost decide to emigrate immediately to Canada."[17] Apparently, the desired results of the promotion efforts fell short of expectations, as only a few Dutchmen were willing to pack their bags for the 'promised land'. Toe Laer blamed this lack of interest primarily on the high cost of passage to Canada.

In spite of various attempts to place Canada in the limelight, it does seem that knowledge and interest about Canada during most of the 19th century was shared by only a very small number of Dutch people. For most, Canada was simply a place somewhere in the vicinity of Niagara Falls, located north of the persistently self-promoting and rapidly-growing United States.

However, for some curious Dutch individuals, Canada had kindled their imaginations, which resulted in the decision that a Canadian excursion could occasionally be included in an itinerary for travel in the United States. This book honours a small number of Dutch travellers to the North American continent who, fortunately, left records both published and unpublished, of their various adventures.

There are also a few travellers who left records that were too limited to be included in the main body of this book. However, to honour and be mindful of their respective journeys to Canada, we shall briefly mention them. Gerard C. Coster,[18] son of the wealthy

Amsterdam merchant Haro Joachim Coster of H. J. Coster & Co., travelled with his servant to his notably wealthy uncle, John G. Coster, in New York. In a letter from Montreal dated February 22, 1831, to his aunt Johanna Smaale de Reus in Amsterdam, he wrote that he had left New York (where he had arrived on November 1,1830) after one month there. He told her that he had also spent the winter months in Montreal. His only reference to Canada was that "Montreal was located in Canada" and "is even colder than Russia". Unfortunately, the intriguing question as to what brought him to Canada remains, so far, unanswered.[19]

Also worth mentioning is the Amsterdam banker, Jan Lodewijk Pierson, who was involved with financing of the CPR. In 1883, he travelled on the CPR line with another Amsterdam banker, his associate Adolphe A. H. Boissevain. They reached the end of the track, the barren spot "without one house built" where Medicine Hat is now situated. Of this experience, he tells of the morning after having slept on the floor of a tent. He was much taken by the empty prairie landscape inhabited by First Nation people. Upon seeing this, he wondered about the wisdom of the initial Dutch investments in the CPR. He also recounts that, of course, ultimately the venture proved to be very successful.[20]

The main body of this book focuses on more extensive narratives written by Dutch men who did not consider Canada home, and who eventually returned home to Holland. One exception is Duke Bernhard of Saxe-Weimar-Eisenach who, although born in Germany, lived for many years in Holland where he dutifully served as a high-ranking officer in the Dutch army. Following these criteria, we collected the stories from a total of fourteen travellers who had visited Canada in the 19th century. Many of them included a trip to Canada along with their tour of the United States. From these works, we only used the parts of their narratives that relate to Canada. They include the literary contributions of the following persons: Willem T. Gevers Deynoot[21] (1860), Gerrit Verschuur[22] (1877), Bernard C. Schuijlenburg[23] (1890), and Cornelis J. Wijnaendts Francken[24] (1891). In 1825–1826, Duke Bernard of Saxe-Weimar-Eisenach travelled to the United States and Canada. He published his story in Germany in 1828. Later that year, an English version was printed in Philadelphia. The following year, a Dutch edition translated from the original German was issued in Dordrecht, the Netherlands.[25] These contributions were mostly written and published by the gentlemen travellers themselves, soon after they had completed their journey.

In contrast, the preserved travel journals of L.R. Koolemans Beijnen, J. R. Mees, Claude August Crommelin and Ernst Sillem were commercially published. The expedition to the Canadian Arctic, as reported by Dutch navy officer, Koolemans Beijnen, was published the year after he had returned home.[26] The part of the expedition's story, which took place in 1875 in Canadian waters, is included. It is with thanks to the good custodianship of a number of Mees' family members that we can read about his journey to Canada. His manuscript about his trip to the United States and Canada in 1843 had been handed down in the family over several generations, and was finally published in 1988.[27] Some years ago, the record of Crommelin's journey through America in 1866–1867, which includes a passage about his six-day visit to Canada, was discovered in a library in St. Paul, Minnesota. The material was annotated and published in 2009.[28] In an almost identical fashion, the eight forgotten travel journals of Ernst Sillem were discovered. In 1996, completely unaware of their existence, a family member stumbled upon them. These journals, published in 1997,[29] chronicle Sillem's trip around the world from 1888–1890. Of Canada, he writes about meeting influential people and his journey by train from Quebec to Victoria.

Not all of the travel records were journals. Klaas J. Kuipers wrote his stories long after he left active service at sea. In his memoirs, he describes his adventures as a seaman, which took him to many parts of the world during the period 1790–1818. In 1811, he visited Canada. From this work published in 1844, we have only used that part of the text dealing with Canada.[30] A letter written in French by Johan C. Gevers, a Dutch diplomat who served in the United States, provides us with a more formal view. After being assigned to a new post in Europe in 1845, he made a short visit to Canada, about which he reported in a letter addressed to his Minister of Foreign Affairs.[31] For Karel D. W. Boissevain, life in Canada was good. The first six months of his stay in Canada were spent in the Rocky Mountains. His writings, containing provocative comments about Canada's political and cultural scenes, first appeared in print in three segments in a Dutch newspaper in 1892.[32] Two letters written by Lodewijk R. J. A. Roosmale Nepveu from Yorkton (in what is now Saskatchewan) about the circumstances of new Dutch immigrants were published October 4 and October 11, 1893 in a Christian weekly, *Het Oosten: weekblad gewijd aan Christelijke philanthropie*. A collection of original letters by Frederik Christiaan Colenbrander tell of his visit with some Dutch immigrants in the area near Yorkton. These letters to his family covering his 1893 journey to North America were preserved and eventually archived as part of a family collection in the Regional Archive in Zutphen in the Netherlands.

It is by virtue of the efforts of these gentlemen, who candidly and prudently recorded their stories that we now have the opportunity to see other versions of the rich history of Canada's past.

Having scanned the last names of the authors, it soon became apparent that the travellers were predominantly members of the Dutch aristocracy, a genteel milieu of established rulers.[33] Some were members of prominent business families, while a few belonged to the Dutch nobility. Therefore, they had both the money and the time to travel. They lived in a class-based society where a Protestant elite dominated a power-base — one could not join unless one was born into it. One would recognize these people by their clothing and mannerisms. Almost all of them were highly educated and were able to contribute through their writings and observations, which of course were influenced by the culture or society they came from. They were men capable of making sharp and incisive observations and evaluations, but not without revealing the prejudices and stereotypes common to their time. These were also gentlemen flushed with confidence, and prepared for travel. They toted travel guides along with their baggage. Being for the most part inquisitive and erudite, they were also not inclined to leave any topic untouched.

Even though almost all of the travellers belonged to the privileged classes, not all were tourists in the common sense of the word. Nevertheless, they all took the opportunity to do some sightseeing during their trips. For most of them, going to Canada meant making the almost obligatory visit to Niagara, which, for the reading public at home, was identified as a 'Natural Wonder'. It was foremost the 'Falls' that local newspapers and travel literature wrote about and the Falls were also seen as being synonymous with Canada. When travelling from the USA to Canada, quite often travellers met up with Americans who were doing the 'North', and consequently, the Falls. However impressive and wonderful the sight might have been to most, the Dutch travellers had mixed feelings about it. There were many words of praise, ranging from "nicer than expected" to "never shall I forget this scene." However, it could not fulfill all the travellers' expectations. The very experienced world traveller Gerrit Verschuur, who made this journey together with his brother Wouter, was awestruck by seeing the huge volume of water, despite having been told beforehand that it could not match the waterfalls in the Yosemite Valley in California, which he had already seen during his trip through the USA. Regardless of his favourable opinion of the Falls, he was dismayed with the shocking manner in which foreigners were being exploited. He told his readers that when visiting the Falls they should keep their hands on their wallets. He warned that every footstep set on the bridge cost 25 cents and that a dozen photographers would follow them around offering a portrait with the Falls in the background.

All the travellers, except for three, visited at least one of the various eastern cities, such as Halifax, Quebec City, Montreal and Toronto. Four of them visited the West, of which two spent a short time in Victoria and Vancouver, while the only Arctic traveller, so far as we know, never set foot in a Canadian city. Coming from the "low lands", all were enthusiastic about the beautiful natural settings of Quebec City and Montreal. Kuiper, who visited Quebec City at the beginning of the 19th century, praised the excellent view of the city located high on a hill, with its main church and high buildings. Down the St. Lawrence was

Montreal with Mount Royal in the background and the gleaming sun on its copper roofs. This view obviously touched the Dutch heartstrings, because it was so different from the cities in Holland with their small houses with baked red roof tiles which had no backdrop of hills. Toronto, which Schuijlenburg called a "small town", passed the test for these mostly urbane Dutchmen — it had a nice outlook, clean streets and lovely shops. Being used to Europe's beautiful buildings, these travellers had an eye for new town planning and noticed the straight and wide streets. They were further impressed and perhaps surprised by the Canadian architecture. They were very much in awe of the "decorative post office in Adelaide Street" in Toronto and the CPR Main office in Montreal, "built in an unknown, but very graceful style". In particular, the dimensions of these buildings, which were much larger in scale than was customary at home, must have sparked the imaginations, even of these men.

Against the overwhelmingly favourable narratives about Canada's cities, only a couple words of dissent were heard. In the opinion of Mees, the streets in Halifax were in a poor state. According to Duke Bernard, the town of Sorel, Quebec, which he visited in 1825, was not in much better shape. He was convinced that this was the case in almost all of the Canadian cities, as compared to those in the USA and he predicted that they would never achieve the same standing. Time has proven him to be utterly wrong, at least in the eyes of Canadians!

It is no exaggeration to suggest that almost all European travellers, including the Dutch, came to North America to see and feel the 'American vitality', a phenomenon they had read and heard so much about. This was supposed to be a force, characterized by the optimistic courage and indomitable will-power necessary to succeed in the battle with natural forces and requiring a great propensity for adaptability. Some travellers also noticed this form of vitality in Canada, although doubtless to a lesser degree than in the USA. The clearing of the land by the pioneers was clearly acknowledged and praised, which led some to predict a great future for Canada. However, here and there were some words of caution about this progress, that is, concerns about the exploitation of

Canada's natural resources. In 1859, demonstrating a fairly modern attitude, Gevers-Deynoot questions the "reckless" way of cutting the forest, the rather crude American and (in his eyes) uncivilized way of taking care of Mother Nature. Gevers-Deynoot who, had persuaded his cousin Claudius F. W. Gevers [34] to join him on this trip, warned his readers that these large cuttings could cause climatic changes and would result in shortages of rain in some places.

Observations about the economic possibilities of the land were not uncommon. With his knowledge of agriculture, Colebrander believed that "this was good land for poor colonists; of course for the first years they have to struggle and work hard, nevertheless one can grow beautiful wheat." The young banker, Ernst Sillem, demonstrated uncanny foresight about the future of Vancouver. In 1888, he wrote that if he did not already have a job, he would have liked to settle in the city to look for his fortune stating, "This is a city in which one can make money". As early as 1890, another learned man, Wijnaendts Francken, already saw a great future for the development of the Banff Hot Springs. He correctly foresaw that they would become a significant tourist destination. Even though he was a biologist by training, and in contrast to Gevers-Deynoot before him, he made no comment about the effect this development could have on the natural habitat.

Another form of the 'American vitality' was the drive and desire to exploit new technologies and innovations, which sparked interest in Holland and about which some of the travellers wrote extensively. For example, one grand structure of engineering that made a profound impression was the Victoria Bridge in Montreal, then the longest bridge in the world. With its 24 ice-breaking pillars and the metal railway tube made of prefabricated sections, Gevers-Deynoot portrayed the bridge as "a masterpiece of architecture". It could withstand both the strong current and the heavy, icy conditions that also prevailed in Holland, a country with a geography that necessitated many bridges and where the temperatures could periodically dip to nasty lows. Mentioning the price tag of $7,000,000, Claude Crommelin too was very much "impressed by its scale".

Originating from a nation of merchants and seafarers, these travellers showed great interest in Canadian ships by commenting about the ships' models and methods of construction. In order to travel through Canada in the early days, one had to take a number of boats on unpredictable waters. As passengers on these various vessels, they reported in great detail about the ships' measurements, the names of the engine makers, and the amount of horsepower delivered. Most were very pleased with the interiors, the cleanliness, the quality of service rendered and the excellent food. In general, they found the ships to be much larger than those in Holland and noted the use of many more steamships, which burned wood instead of coal, as was utilized at home. New technological developments had motivated King Willem I[35] to request that Duke Bernard survey these inventions during a trip to America. The Dutch government was particularly interested in new military and naval technology, but the Duke also inspected the products of civil engineering such as bridges and dykes. Being both highly educated and well-informed given his position, he discovered a little secret while inspecting navy ships in the harbour of Kingston. That is, the British fleet that anchored in the Kingston harbour apparently carried too much firepower, which was, alleged by the Duke, to be in contravention of the Treaty of Ghent. He likely should have referred to the Rush-Bagot Agreement between Canada and the United States which limited naval forces on the Great Lakes along the international border following the War of 1812.[36] To assist the Duke during his travels in making records of the sophisticated technology, the King had authorized a naval engineer August E. Tromp, to travel with the Duke and provide him with an extensive report. This exceptionally detailed document, intended for the Minister of the Navy, is filled with detailed descriptions of North American water management technology, including technical drawings. It also contains detailed specifications of several Canadian vessels.[37]

Even though the Industrial Revolution had also influenced and reshaped parts of the fabric of Dutch society, in the latter part of the 19th century, agriculture still accounted for a major part of the Dutch economy. However, competition from large wheat-growing countries outside of Europe was on the horizon. Dutch farmers followed from a distance the new North American harvesting techniques in the various trade magazines and in the national press. While travelling in Canada, Schuijlenburg noticed the use of peculiar agricultural implements and remembered reading about it. The most fascinating and important to him was seeing the mowing of hay "in the twinkling of an eye" by a row of 20 modern cutting machines. In describing this scene he was perhaps hinting to his readers that agriculture in Holland was destined to change.

During the 19th century, people in Holland had probably heard of or read about 'Black' people and 'Indians'. It is more likely that since they did not appear on the streets in Holland, they remained more or less a mystery to most Dutch people. It is therefore not surprising that the judgments in general expressed about these peoples included the negative prejudices of the time. The travellers in this book were generally mild in their judgments and in some aspects, relatively positive. Mees, who had seen black people during his stay in the United States, was completely surprised to see black soldiers in Toronto who, as he put it, were neatly dressed and seemed to be happy. Gevers Deynoot seemed to exhibit a more liberal view, showing some degree of sympathy for black people, during an event that took place in Clifton House at a time when slavery had been abolished in all the British Colonies but not in all of the American states.[38] Duke Bernard, on the other hand expressed not so much a liberal view, as a fascination with personalities. With much respect and, yes, perhaps with furtive adoration, he wrote about a Mrs. Grymes,[39] a Creole lady from Louisiana whom he had met while coming from the United States.

In the 19th century when 'Indians' were generally portrayed as lazy and evasive, the Dutch travellers indicated quite a different outlook and did not make such harsh judgements. For example, Verschuur's tone is very positive when he notes, "they are good-natured and allow us to enter their dwellings." This tone was echoed by some of the Dutch travellers who, perhaps to their great surprise, showed acknowledgement and respect for the Indian pilots. These pilots safely navigated the large passenger ships through the St. Lawrence rapids.

Most of the travellers entered Canada from the United States and by so doing, they were able in some aspects to compare life in Canada with that of the country to the south. Gevers saw a great difference in the standard of living between the two. Mees' only criticism was that the service provided in hotels in the United States was better than he had experienced in Canada. Schuijlenburg, on the other hand, seems to have had a more favourable view of Canada. He noticed that, in comparison to the United States, the stores in Montreal were open much longer and possessed an enjoyable ambiance, probably produced by a more French or European interior. Verschuur expressed a frank dislike for Americans and considered French-Canadians to be the most polite and hospitable people, in sharp contrast to the Yankees.

About the country itself, some remarked on the difference in prosperity between Lower and Upper Canada. They noted a great discrepancy between what they called the mainly French-populated areas with those that was primarily settled by British and Scottish people. Lower Canada's overt poverty was blamed on the influence of Catholic priests who they believed kept the French population superstitious and ignorant. The Irish population were also considered a negative factor and, according to Gevers, unsuitable as colonists. These types of comments about Catholics were prevalent in the 19th century and were not just espoused by the Protestant elite. Upper Canada was mainly populated by people of the Protestant faith and was more prosperous. This seems to correspond with the ideas that most of the travellers held about Protestants and their legendary work ethic. Verschuur held the minority view. He did not express any critical comments about the French Canadians, instead he showed great admiration for them.

Perhaps somewhat predictably, the topic to which the most pen and paper was dedicated was the natural landscape of Canada. The country's natural splendour runs as a common thread through all the narratives. It is plausible that for a number of the travellers, the journey to Canada was largely inspired by the desire to see

Niagara Falls. It would not be a great stretch to assume that what they remembered the most after returning home were the Falls and other natural features: the lakes, mountains, forests and the vastness of the high north, all of which symbolized so much of Canada. Coming from a small and highly organized country, it must have amazed them to find that it took a minimum of 52 hours by steamer to reach Montreal from Niagara Falls in 1850.

Comparisons with Europe were inevitable. Travelling on the large lakes was explained to Dutch readers as sailing "on open Seas", some of the Great Lakes being bigger in surface area than Holland itself! On the other side of Canada, the surroundings of Glacier Station on the CPR line in the Rockies understandably drew much praise, touted as a landscape that was as beautiful as any found in Switzerland. For that matter, the West Coast, which Wijnaendts Francken visited at the end of 19th century, reminded him of many parts of Europe and he gave his readers a fair indication of how Canada appeared at that period in time. Most travellers revered the great St. Lawrence River. Its shores were also compared with those of the Italian lakes and its surroundings with the area around Nice. Verschuur was also touched by the splendour of the St. Lawrence, saying it "gave me bliss", in stark contrast with having been on the Mississippi, an experience which had "left him cold". Many of the travellers wrote about the Lachine rapids, which one described as "a must one had to see". It is understandable that the travellers admired the rivers, and wanted to inform their readers about them, since these rivers were so different from those at home.

Discussions about nature invariably included a few comments about the weather. Roosmale Nepveu's account of the climate on the Prairies is particularly positive. "It is very warm here, but the nights are cold. You never see a cloud in the sky. It is clearly noticeable that this is a different climate and a much more cheerful one than ours." Only Boissevain, while travelling on the CPR, relays in poetic form his experience of a heavy snowfall on the Prairies and the lovely winter street in Montreal. He had no problem with Montreal's winter. As a man who was born of the damp peat ground, polders and canals, he praised the climate of "this northern and sunny land, a source of pleasure and admiration". Koolemans Beijnen, the Dutch Arctic explorer, experienced the most extreme and, arguably, the most beautiful natural forces. His moving story about the precarious situation of being trapped by unexpected fog and ice in early September did not stop him from returning the following year to see once again the splendour of the northern landscape, with its high cliffs and picturesque inlets.

Most travellers wrote at length about the St. Lawrence, the established cities and, of course, the Falls. To prevent the book from becoming a string of repetitive writings and similar observations of the same cities and Niagara Falls, we have created a single journey that takes the reader from Montreal to Niagara Falls and back via Quebec City and its surrounding area. For this, we excerpted what we believe to be the most interesting sections from the various writings and then wove them together as a single tale about a tour of the Great Lakes and vicinity.

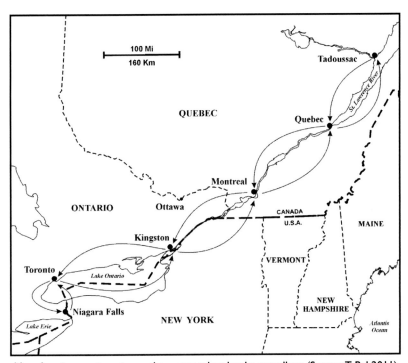

Map showing most routes as they were taken by the travellers. (Source: T. Bal 2011)

During the 19th century, Montreal was, for most travellers, the most interesting large city to visit. It had been called 'The Paris of the North' and was therefore a favourite subject to write about. Because of its popularity and significance for Canada, we have included the musings of a few of the travellers on their most interesting and various descriptions of Montreal and her people.

Four of these stories may have special significance to anyone interested in Western Canadian history. It was not until after the West was opened with the completion of the Canadian Pacific Railway in the early 1880s that travel of the kind already experienced in eastern Canada was possible. Two of these stories are about trips on the CPR to Canada's west coast and, of course, the Rocky Mountains. The others refer to Dutch immigration to the Yorkton, Saskatchewan area. The final chapter is Kooleman Beijnen's suspense-filled tale of the *Pandora's* laborious trek through the icy waters of the Canadian Arctic, following the route of the ill-fated 1845 Franklin expedition.

The first of the collected stories in this book is from Jan R. Mees. On his way to the USA, he made a scheduled stop in Halifax. His short but unique exposé, taking us to the eastern-most harbour town as it was in 1843, gave us the right place to begin.

This book is not a strictly chronological history, since each of these travellers wrote about their experiences at different moments in time. We are satisfied that the excerpted material provides a fair representation of their respective thoughts and impressions. Altogether, this is a story which not only gives us a unique description of the countryside but which also allows us, time and again, to share in delightful and sometimes frankly unfavourable comments about Canada's inhabitants. Interest in these people was perhaps one reason that impelled the Dutch to travel here and which of course remains to this day a primary reason for anyone to visit foreign lands.

CANADA

Crown of her, young Vancouver; crest of her, old Quebec;

Atlantic and far Pacific sweeping her, keel to deck.

North of her, ice and arctics; southward a rival's stealth;

Aloft, her Empire's pennant; below, her nation's wealth.

Daughter of men and markets, bearing within her hold,

Appraised at highest value, cargoes of grain and gold.

Emily Pauline Johnson

Chapter One
Halifax, 1843

Jan R. Mees

The journey to North America during the 19th century for most Dutch travellers started by ship, sailing directly from Europe to a harbour in the United States. Consequently their Canadian tours commenced at the various United States–Canada border crossings, like the ones near Detroit, Buffalo or the state of Vermont. It is fortuitous, then, to find one story of a traveller to America in 1843 who sailed directly to Halifax then continued to the city of Boston. Jan Rudolf Mees, the 25-year-old scion of a Rotterdam business family, crossed the Atlantic to tour the United States and Canada. Only a few years before, Halifax had become an important port of entry for immigrants and travellers because of its shipping links to Great Britain. In 1840, the first scheduled connection was established between Liverpool, Halifax, Boston and Quebec City. The company was officially called the British and North American Royal Mail Steam Packet Company, founded by Canadian-born Samuel Cunard. Cunard's first steamship, the *Britannia*, was launched in 1840. It was the very same vessel that Mees sailed on as a high-paying cabin-class passenger. As the ship approached the Halifax harbour, Mees made some interesting observations about local maritime customs. The short stop in Halifax allowed the ship to refuel, drop off and pick up passengers, and load the ever-important mail. Mees took the opportunity during this short stopover to wander around the town, leading to some pointed and uncompromising views about the economic and social situation in Halifax, as well as about some of its inhabitants.

"Friday, 14 April, 1843, Distance 198 miles, latitude 43° 54', longitude 48° on the banks of Newfoundland, where it was very cold. The sea was very calm, therefore we made 9 to 10 knots, wind W S W, however very light. I have seen two anchored barks.

Saturday, April 15, distance 254, latitude 43° 44', longitude 59° 30 wind SW, mild breeze, everything was under early evening fog. At midnight, according to calculations, we were near the coast, therefore tacking back and forth. But since the fog was very thick on Monday morning the 17th, we laid at anchor until 7 a.m. when it cleared; we saw the coast of Nova Scotia in front of us at a distance of 5 to 6 miles, which looked very bad, since one could clearly see the snow on the hills. A few shots were fired to call for a pilot, but since, according to calculations, we had to be a few miles north of Halifax, we sailed southwards along the southern coast, where we soon noticed the pilot, who came on board at 9hr 15 minutes.

Halifax from Dartmouth, 1842

The pilot boats from Halifax are no more than four-oar wherries. We continued the same course and arrived after about thirteen days journey in total from the time we departed England, at 10 o'clock at the quay in Halifax. The entrance to the Halifax harbour is easily accessible, the city being situated in a spacious bay where, even close to the city, the average depth of the water is 16 fathoms. The entryway is very beautiful. Both shores of the bay are high. The city is built against a hill, located on the south side near a small stream that flows in the bay. Before one gets to the city, one passes a small island with fortifications, which are also present on the mainland, so that the city is completely protected.

We said goodbye to the passengers who left us in Halifax, several of whom were destined for St. John, New Brunswick. Then we went on shore with permission for three hours, which time was used to visit the city, which is otherwise nothing special. On the whole, it had a rather dirty appearance partially contributed to by the unfavourable weather which one has had to encounter lately. The snow was still on the ground in different places, and on the roads further inland, the snow is still so deep that the mailbags for Boston have not arrived as yet. The houses are mainly constructed from wood and painted white, however it appeared from a few buildings that in the vicinity there was very nice granite, mostly very speckled. There are about 18,000 residents. A large part of their livelihood is fishing and fisheries and some trade with the West Indies. We visited the fortification or Citadel, which is well-built, located on a hill behind the city. We walked through the underground corridors, being at least a mile long. There are many blacks and a number of Indians from the Micmac tribe, who settled here before European colonization. They are good-looking people; amongst them are many beautiful women. I saw only one British warship. However, there are many military men, mainly engineers. It has been said to be a pleasant town. After having walked for quite some time through the mud, we returned at one o'clock to our vessel, a change for the better. The streets seemed to me in a poor state.

We were soon again at sea and kept the pilot on board. In exchange for twelve passengers that had left us, twenty new ones had come on board in Halifax destined for Boston. They were for the most part, Bluenoses, a nickname that is given to the people of Nova Scotia.

Amongst them were strange characters, wearing waist-length jackets of duffel, which seemed to be very much worn. Overall, one associated very little with them. The original passengers, completely wrongly in my view, saw them as intruders."

Chapter Two
From the USA border to Montreal, 1843

Jan R. Mees

For years, many travellers coming from the United States to Canada crossed the border from Lake Champlain in the state of Vermont by ship, as did Jan Rudolf Mees who had made an extensive journey through the United States. He had travelled as far south as Virginia where he inspected some family business interests, and entered Canada for a scenic boat trip on board the *Burlington*. After disembarking and once again on Canadian soil, Mees continued his journey by both rail and boat towards Montreal, the starting point of his Canadian tour. This stretch took him through flat land, which sparked reminiscences and comparisons with the landmarks and landscapes at home, a more or less automatic response of any traveller.

The *Burlington*

"At three o'clock p.m. we boarded the *Burlington*, arriving from Whitehall and destined for St. Jean, Canada, located at the top of Lake Champlain. This lake is vast and fairly wide in the centre. The water is not as clear as Lake George and the shores, although hilly, are lower. At first it seems that Lake George is pleasant enough, however, because of the presence of cities on the shores and many small ships, Lake Champlain is more varied. The steamboat, *Burlington*, is known all over the country because it is neat and in good condition. Order and neatness prevails in the smallest detail to a degree I have never experienced on board a steamboat. Commands are not shouted; everything works through bell rings and the good order extends so far that sailors and stewards wear a kind of uniform. The bunks are just as good as in a hotel. Captain Sherman is always present in the boat when passengers are set off or picked up, and this happens so swiftly that almost no time is lost. The Captain's cabin is on the upper deck, where a piano stands ready for the ladies to use. He is very courteous to them. At seven o'clock in the evening, we moored for a short while at the town of Burlington, in the state of Vermont. Although, it was already getting dark, I saw enough to see that the city was uninteresting. Yet its location is extremely beautiful. Because of a quiet evening and a clear moon, we had a pleasant journey and arrived at eight o'clock in the morning in St. Jean, a few hours later than scheduled, because we were forced to stop for three hours due to fog. At some distance from Burlington, the passage is very narrow and the land on the Canadian side is low and barren. Here and there, one sees a house in the marshes occupied by fishermen, whom one can frequently see seated in canoes in the water. They wore rather pointy toques and one immediately detects a change in the appearance of people when one comes from the States; it is an unhealthy region. One passes a few British fortresses before one arrives at St. John. One is not really on Lake Champlain anymore, but rather on the Sorel or Richelieu River, which carries the water from the lake to the St. Lawrence. The length of Lake Champlain is 125 miles. St. John is an insignificant town and the customs officers were not difficult when examining the luggage. After breakfast, we left by railroad for La Prairie, which is located seventeen miles away by steamboat from Montreal, where we arrived at noon on August 11. The countryside between St. John and La Prairie is entirely flat *and I had not seen such landscape since my departure from Holland. Moreover, along the St. Lawrence is a low dike. Unlike the Dutch landscape, however, the land is not well cultivated and there are no windmills. From La Prairie one sees Montreal at a distance of about three miles. And nearing the city, the eye catches the shining roofs, mostly on the large buildings, which creates a nice effect when the sun shines on them. And the sun not only shone on the roofs of Montreal but also on the streets. Since there is no tree to be seen on the quay along the river, the sun shone also on the passengers of the steamboat on their way to the hotel. It had not been as hot here for a long time. With some others, I quartered in an English hotel that was all right as far as the food and rooms were concerned. The service was bad, which one especially notices when one comes from the United States where in good hotels, orderly service is more prevalent."*

Montreal, 1859

Willem T. Gevers-Deynoot

Willem T. Gevers-Deynoot   Claudius F.W. Gevers

Mees' less-than-positive comments about Montreal, contrast clearly with those of Willem Theodore Gevers-Deynoot. During his tour in 1859 through Canada, he had come to Montreal together with his cousin Claudius Frederik Willem Gevers. Both gentlemen, who were part of the Dutch nobility, had arrived in Canada also via the state of Vermont. Gevers-Deynoot had come to America and Canada, as he explained in the foreword of his book, to "inform the people at home about these lands". This was his obligation to Dutch people, perhaps prompted by the fact that at that time he was a member of the Dutch Lower House.[40] He showed himself to be both a keen observer and an eloquent writer who provided an interesting and upbeat account of Montreal. He was very excited about seeing the construction of the Victoria Bridge, at that time an engineering sensation that must have also been of great interest to his readers in Holland. Having crossed into Canada at the American border, and while sailing further on a steamboat in the St. Lawrence towards Montreal, Gevers-Deynoot started his description of Montreal.

> *"Its many lights were visible at a half-hour distance across the river. After having arrived there, the carriages of the different hotels having stood by, we stepped out at the Donegana Hotel where we rejoiced with a good supper, being served by a number of Negroes.*
>
> *We are now in Canada, and I will, before we go further, remind my readers of a thing or two about this landscape: Canada is an Indian name, which in Iroquois means 'gathering of huts'. It is known that Canada was firstly discovered in 1497. The first European settlement took place in 1541, by a certain Jacques Cartier, a Frenchman, who sailed up the St. Lawrence River, giving it its name. Not until 1608, however was the colony somewhat enlarged, when the French established the city of Quebec, etc. From that time until 1759, the whole region remained under French rule. On September 13 of that year, Quebec was taken by the English army under General Wolfe. Shortly afterward, all of Canada that had carried the name "New France" was ceded to the English crown.*
>
> *Since then, this part of North America (that is extremely large and counts for almost half of its northern part) remained a British*

possession. Her prominent provinces are Canada West and Canada East, New Brunswick and Nova Scotia. The last two regions are, for the greater part, forested. In Canada, the area alongside both shores of the St. Lawrence River is the most cultivated. The rest is still wilderness for the most part.

Canada is governed by a Governor General, appointed by the English crown, and has a legislative body, the provincial parliament, which holds session in Quebec. This parliament is split into two chambers. The members of the Senate are appointed for life by the English crown; the people elect the other chamber. This form of government was adopted after 1840, since the French and English elements that always distinguish Canada East from Canada West sparked of extensive conflicts. With compliance and prudent negotiation by English statesmen, a union of Canada with the United States was prevented.

The climate of Canada is similar with that of Sweden and St. Petersburg, however located at lower northern latitude. The winters are long and cold; the summer is short but generally very hot, while in Canada West, the climate is in general much milder than in Canada East, attributed to its close vicinity to the large lakes. The last region, where Quebec and Montreal are located, is very mountainous and forested, and provides the tourist with more natural beauty than the first. Canada West's surface is level, and therefore, also more fertile. The wild Ottawa River, a bit above Montreal, separates both provinces.

The roots laid down by the first French settlement are strong, especially in Canada East. A large number of the populace still speaks French. In both Montreal and Quebec one sees French signboards and the street names are written both in French and in English. In many villages, not only the names, but the outward appearance of the inhabitants also reveals their French heritage, especially from Normandy. We had hardly set foot on Canadian soil when the following immediately caught our eyes. Along the railway, one beholds the 'traverse du chemin de fer', and at the stations one could hear the people chat in French. We heard many complaints; the French component is too old-fashioned and passive and does not know how to go along with the industrious spirit of progress demonstrated by the English and the Americans. That is also why Canada West is more developed than Canada East. Therefore, I believe, by the nature of things, that sooner or later it will be overwhelmed and dissolved by dominant English.

As I have said, having stopped off in Montreal at the Donegana Hotel, we spent the next day visiting the city and the surrounding area. Montreal is a city of about 60,000 residents, situated on a large island in the St. Lawrence River. She derives her name from a hill that stands behind the city [Mount Royal] and is dotted with country houses, gardens and trees. From there one enjoys an impressive view of the city and the wide river. The location of Montreal is beautiful. It has a very long brickwork quay along the river, where a number of large seagoing vessels and steamships were moored. On that side, one also discovers a number of attractive public buildings constructed of greyish stone but the city centre was rather disappointing. Built

Donegana Hotel, 1860

in 1640, a part of Montreal still has some small wooden houses that look somewhat seedy. A few wide streets cut the city lengthwise. The layout is extremely spacious, so one finds a number of open spaces that still have to be developed. The city does seem to expand quickly, and many new houses are being erected. The Roman Catholic faith has the upper hand, for which a new cathedral was built. There are number of monasteries; most of them are allied with benevolent societies. On a small plaza, a dilapidated memorial for Nelson is displayed.

In many aspects, Montreal has Nordic character, which one finds in Sweden and Northern Russia. The spires and many house roofs are covered with sheets of zinc, iron or tin. When the sun shines upon them, it gives the city a glistening appearance. Many streets and neighborhoods have all wooden paving.

There is much trade because fully-loaded ships can sail up the St. Lawrence, which is connected to western and southern North America by canals and railways. The total in aggregate sales of furs is substantial. I was also amazed by the industry, which is achieved through a number of factories. We found an English military garrison, artillery and infantry; and from a fortress beside the city one could hear the morning and evening salute. All things considered, it was evident that we were not in the big Republic [USA] anymore.

Most remarkable is Montreal's Victoria Bridge, which will link both shores of the wide St. Lawrence. This bridge is in the western part of the city and is almost completed.[41] It is said that up to now it will be longest bridge built, and is financed with English capital. It is a tubular iron bridge that rests on twenty-five arches. The middle arch is 330 feet long; the twenty-four others are each 242 feet long. The approach to each side of the bridge is 242 feet long, and her whole length amounts to 7,000 feet. The vertical measurement of the centre arch above the river measures sixty feet. The iron tube for the steam trains is twenty-two feet high and sixteen feet wide. Three million cubic feet weight of stone and 8,000 tons of iron will be used for the bridge. She will cost more than two million dollars. Although the ice in the river sometimes builds up to five feet thick or more, there are no icebreakers in front of the bridge, because the piers are made up of thick bricks and are wedge-shaped at the top. Every column must withstand the pressure of 70,000 tons of ice.

Because of her monumental dimensions, the Victoria Bridge appears striking, but she is also ponderous and uninspiring. What most impressed me is how they succeeded in making a secure connection in the strong currents of the St. Lawrence. Not too far above Montreal, the wide Ottawa River unloads itself with full force into the St. Lawrence. Both merge and now stream together with formidable speed between the arches of the bridge. The speed is so great that far away below Montreal, the waters of both rivers are still separate and one can clearly see the murky water of the Ottawa River stream alongside the clear green water of the St. Lawrence.[42]

St. Helen's Island, that is mainly used as a military depot, a bit below Montreal, splits the river into two parts.

In the city, I met Indians in their traditional costume for the first time. They were small in stature, yellow-faced, with long black downward-hanging hair, and were colourfully dressed.

Centre Tube Victoria Bridge, 1869

Noteworthy was the large number of rental carriages, small closed wagons called 'vehicles', harnessed with a horse and seating four people on two benches opposite each other.

I shall mention another curious event that came to pass in our hotel (and which one encounters in many North American hotels).

It is about the servants, serving in a synchronized way at dinner. This is a strange sight, at first. To explain, before the dinner starts and the guests are seated (they are normally seated at long tables, or at small tables for eight, ten or twelve persons) a group of servants, mostly Negroes, each with a main dish, line up behind the tables. At a given signal, they all put dishes in front of the guests. After another sign, they lift the lids (which are usually metal) with much din and take them away in a queue. Thereafter, the serving starts. The taking away and the dishing up of each dish occurs in the same rehearsed way. It is said it is done to create more orderliness at the tables. Since we were now on English territory, the bill was not only presented in dollars and cents, but also in pounds sterling and shillings. On average, however, the prices were the same in Canada as in the United States.

Lastly, I should mention that we visited a ménagerie with live animals in Montreal which, despite being poorly exhibited, contained very nice examples of the animal world. Those that especially attracted our attention belonged to the northern part of America. We saw bison, panthers, bears, deer, beavers and a few snakes."

Chapter Three
Montreal – Kingston, 1859

Willem T. Gevers-Deynoot

Even though Montreal had its unique features and attractions for the travellers, the highlight of the journey to Canada for most of them was a visit to the mighty Niagara Falls. To get there from Montreal required a lengthy boat trip. The first leg of this journey would go along the St. Lawrence with a stop at the little village of Prescott and from there to Kingston. During a stopover in Kingston, passengers would be given time for a walkabout, which gave them a chance to make some observations about the former capital. Soon after the ready-bell for departure had rung, Gevers-Deynoot, who travelled with his cousin C.F.W. Gevers, headed out from Montreal on the *Banshee* toward Kingston.

> *"Straightaway, we steamed at half-speed into a channel that was separated from the St. Lawrence by locks. The repeated mooring and locking was rather difficult, although the latter went quickly. The channel seemed to me to be well-constructed; the locks were solid, constructed completely from stacks of thick, bare tree trunks. We sailed in the midst of a very industrial region, which surrounds Montreal on this side. The city with her hill, also seen from here, gives a nice impression. We finally entered the river again, which was very wide and looked like a lake; the banks were low but forested. Here and there, one saw a small island covered with pine trees. Soon, we entered*

another channel, the Lachine, where a village also bearing that name is located. From Lachine, one sees Kahnawake, an Indian village, which has embraced the Roman Catholic faith, and is engaged with pilot ships and rafts down to Montreal. To me, the region looked rocky, poor and unproductive. I was assured, however, that the latter is not the case, but that the appearance must be put down to the uneducated habitants, being farmers, descendents of French colonists, who settled here.

We still had to lock through five channels this day and the following night, all built to circumvent the fast stream, and by which one rises 200 feet. For the journey downstream, however, the steamboats will not use these channels. During the time we were locking, we noticed one of these ships, sailing down the Lachine Rapids. The ship was being swept down with a tearing speed, like through a swirling ocean. Four men were at the rudder and navigated with extreme cautiousness, since, with the smallest strike against the rocks in the riverbed, the vessel would be an irretrievable loss.

On the Banshee, everything was very well-equipped. At eight o'clock in the morning, breakfast was announced with a gong, at 1:30 p.m. dinner, and at 6 o'clock tea or supper. From Montreal onwards, we counted only thirty passengers, which was not un-pleasant for me. Also, there were a few ladies making music in the evening and the time was spent reading and conversing. The vessel was a bit smaller than the Quebec and was also fired with wood that now and then had to be taken in from the riverbanks. As far as rescue goes, in case of misfortune, one found below deck on the ceiling, a number of life preservers made of cork and piping or airless tin drums. When buckled on, one could safely jump in the water. Moreover, in each cabin are also two such appliances and, on this ship, even the seats were fitted as life preservers. On most North American steamships, I found such safety measures and in some states the number of appliances was regulated by government measures, which one could read on a placard in the largest cabin.

The loveliest weather heightened our journey. About the striking scenes that the sunset and sunrise give in America, I shall not speak, in order to come back to it during our trip on the Mississippi. On Thursday, we arrived early in the morning in Prescott, where we stopped for half an hour to wait for passengers arriving from the train. Prescott is a small town that consists mostly of wooden houses and the streets are unpaved. From here, we started our journey on the St. Lawrence in the midst of the so-called Thousand Islands. We had been told so many nice things about them, that they somewhat disappointed us. The river is dotted for a long stretch with large and small islands, all covered with pine trees, among which the ship meanders. A number of picturesque landscapes are created. Because of this, the various shades of the blue-coloured river, the grey rocks and the green pine trees showed up well. It reminded me somewhat of Lake Mälar near Stockholm in Sweden, but I found it rather monotonous.

Towards the evening, we arrived in Kingston, a city of 16,000 residents and formerly the capital of this part of Canada. It was established in 1783 by the English and, from a military point of view, is also a particularly important place. A fortress protects the city. There, one also finds military depots for the British navy. There is quite a lot of commerce. The city is crosscut by spacious, straight streets and has a few public buildings, all built from granite. But, like everywhere else in Canada, they are too disproportionately large."

Military College Kingston, 1890

Chapter Four
Kingston – Niagara, 1859

Willem T. Gevers-Deynoot

The journey toward the mighty Niagara Falls took Gevers-Deynoot and his cousin further westwards on Lake Ontario towards the city of Toronto. During a short interval, which required a transfer of passengers to another ship, they took the opportunity to wander around the already bustling city, commenting on its location as well as showing great foresight about its future. After another safe boat trip, both men disembarked at Youngstown, N.Y. From there a short train ride would take them finally to the village of Niagara Falls.

"From Kingston, we left the St. Lawrence to steam into Lake Ontario. The lake looked like a sea, except that we could see only the Canadian coast on our right hand. We faced headwind so that by the night the ship started to pitch somewhat.

In contrast, daybreak the next morning started most beautifully. The lake was as smooth as glass. One saw various small schooners, which, with their full white sails, tried very slowly to reach the destination of their journey. The Canadian coast was not high but dotted with pine trees.

At about 7:30 p.m., we saw Toronto in front of us, where we soon disembarked.

Toronto is the most important city of Western Canada and has a population of about 50,000 souls. Sixty years ago this site was only occupied by to Indian huts. The development that took place here is unmatched elsewhere in Canada. The city is attractively located on the lake, has wide straight streets and various nice public buildings. There is considerable hustle and bustle in Toronto and it has an inestimably rich future. We were allowed to stay only briefly, in order to transfer from the Banshee *to another steamship, the* Zimmerman, *which would finally take us to the goal of our journey.*

So then we steamed straight across Lake Ontario to Niagara, which took two-and-a-half hours. Lake Ontario, despite being the smallest of the five Great Lakes (which are located in this part of North America) is nevertheless estimated to have a surface of 5,400 square miles. Its deepest point is 600 feet. It is rich in fish and is also one of the first-rate waterways for trade and industry. A number of steamboats and vessels cut across its waters. It is mainly replenished from the higher lakes and by the Niagara River directly from Lake Erie. Since Lake Erie is located 334 feet above Lake Ontario, a twenty-eight mile-long channel [the Welland Canal], equipped with thirty brick and mortar locks, services the shipping world.

Our gigantic Zimmerman *steamed quickly, so that we soon had the mouth of the Niagara River in front of us. On the left was an American fortress that was built at a holdout point in the state of New York. On the right is the Canadian village, Niagara, which counts 3,000 residents.*

Here ended our steamboat journey and we went ashore to immediately take a seat on the Ontario–Erie Railway. In three-quarters of an hour, it would take us to Clifton House near the ever-so-famous Niagara Falls. Very soon thereafter, the train steamed away. Even before the train stopped, I had already heard and discovered through the forest, the majestic natural spectacle that drew us here. In Clifton House, we found an excellent lodge and hoped to stay a few pleasant days at this remarkable place in America."

Chapter Five

Niagara Falls – Horseshoe – American Falls, 1859

Willem T. Gevers-Deynoot

Directly upon arrival, Gevers-Deynoot and his cousin had checked himself in at the nearby-located Clifton House Hotel. This elegant and renowned hotel with its three verandas and large ballroom with crystal chandeliers for many years accommodated the well-to-do tourists. From here, it was only a short distance on foot to the Horseshoe Falls, a scene Gevers-Deynoot found difficult to describe, but one about which he fervently wished to provide a careful explanation for his readers.

"Before I continue with my travel notes, I may explain to my readers that here we approach one of the most difficult chapters presented until now. It is already a difficult task to give an accurate opinion of a region, or even a city. This is even more so of the spectacular activities that take place here. In addition, there are already so many descriptions of the Niagara Falls that I would only repeat myself again. I shall try, briefly and simply, to share one and the other about it and relay the impressions, which we absorbed here.

The Niagara River, separating the United States from Canada, streams, as is known, out of Lake Erie into Lake Ontario, but about halfway between both lakes, hurls itself more than 160 feet straight down and in that way forms the world-famous waterfalls. The first European who discovered them in 1678 was a French Jesuit, Father

Hennepin. The name 'Niagara' is Indian, and in Iroquois means, 'tumbling waters'.

Table Rock Museum and Clifton House, 1859

The falls are split into two, the so-called 'American Falls', which is rectilinear, and the Canadian, which is shaped in the form of a horseshoe. It is so formed, because just above the fall the river is split in two parts by an island called Goat or Iris Island. Below the fall, the Niagara flows with high speed for seven miles through a steep valley until Queenston, where it bends leftwards, to flow quietly a little further into Lake Ontario. It is said that this valley is created by the continuous retreat of the fall resulting from the scouring water over 35,000 years. It is also estimated that the falls still retreat one foot each year, which is very much dependent on the hardness of the rock formation over which the water crashes down. Someday the falls could reach Lake Erie, but before then, the big cataract would fade away, because the riverbed is composed of softer elements. It is calculated that every hour, 100 million tons of water crashes down and, therefore, it is sometimes felt forty-four miles away in Toronto.

With this description in mind, I departed Clifton House and saw the tumbling waterfalls in front of me. The first impression is not as spectacular as one would expect. This is firstly because one is still too far away from the falls, and secondly, because Goat Island is wider than one imagines by reading the map. Hence the falls separate too much and also one actually looks upon the falls from too high a view. Our first job was to get as close as possible to the Canadian Falls, the Horseshoe, and especially to also try to get down to its foot. It was at noon in beautiful summer weather. As we got closer, we ended up deeper into the mist that continuously dampens the surroundings of the falls. We descended along a stairway carved into the rocks, followed a small path in the deep valley and advanced as far as possible to the foot of the falls. Exhilarating and wild was the scene that unrolled in front of us. The horseshoe-shaped fall, which is 2,000 feet wide and 154 feet high, showed itself in all its greatness.

The clear green water, pushed into a large arc, plunged straight down in front of our feet.[43] *Due to the tremendous force onto the rocks, it appeared to bubble and steam and spouted a thick mist high up, which gave off a fine drizzle in all directions. The ground shook and the roar of the plunging water was nearly impossible to bear. Just a few steps further and it was as if the water rebounding against the high rock wall caused a vacuum that took ones breath away. One stood in a thick rain and was repeatedly shaken by heavy wind gusts and felt overcome by dizziness.*

On the left one saw, at some distance, the American Falls in all its majestic form and behind them the frothing and fuming Niagara, streaming very rapidly through her own deeply sunken valley. Never shall I forget this scene. No matter how many different points from which we later viewed those falls, nowhere was this place surpassed.

We stood here under the so-called Table Rock that eroded by the down-pouring water, protruded her wide sharp ends far above our heads. For that reason, this place and the Table Rock from where one looks from above upon the fall, is not without danger. This is because the rock is composed of soft limestone and now and then large masses break free, crashing downwards. According to my judgment, at this point, still greater disasters can occur and even the houses built not far from the edge could be in danger one day.

Being stunned and overwhelmed by the exhilarating drama, we climbed up again over a slippery path to see the falling water from there also. The view from here is, just like at all waterfalls, however majestic, less striking. The wide arm of the Niagara rolls in a large bend, along a sloping path with uncontrollable speed and the waters inevitably plunge down. The rainbows, which materialize above the Falls, were most beautiful.

Not far from the shore, a number of small inns with belvederes are built, which one can climb without having to pay. As well there are stores with Indian and other curiosities. Walking back to our hotel, I noticed a written sign at the edge of Table Rock. It recounted that in 1844, while picking a flower, a fourteen year-old girl had tumbled down 164 feet and was crushed.

Once we had visited the falls on the Canadian side, we now decided to visit them the next day on the American side.

After having visited the Horseshoe Falls the next exciting step for both gentlemen was a visit to the American falls at the other side of the river.

To do this, one had to descend into the deep valley of the Niagara. There was a sloop used as a ferryboat to take the passengers across for a fixed price. One is about a quarter-hour away from the Horseshoe and almost opposite the American Falls. There, the speed of the Niagara is amazing. With great care, one pulled a good oar along the rocky shore. The sloop is turned into the stream and flies, dancing on the waves, swiftly to the other side, with the water spraying directly into our eyes.

Here is a steep staircase of some one hundred steps and beside it a slope, along which a small wagon is hauled upwards by means of waterpower and a cable. After this, we took a seat and were on top in a few minutes. Soon one arrives in the village, Niagara, that is spread out, but where large hotels are built to put up the many visitors to the waterfalls. Straightaway, we went over an ingenious bridge built over a fast-flowing stream, to the previously mentioned Goat or Iris Island, in order to first see the American Falls from underneath, and then afterward to also see the Canadian falls from there.

In order to do the former, one descends by a spiral staircase contained in a wooden cover, then follows a slippery path along the foot of the rock wall and finally arrives underneath the fall. I also experienced here the same sensations I described before, and hung instinctively onto the rocks in order not to be flung down. This waterfall is 900 feet wide and its water plunges 163 feet straight down.

At the Horseshoe Fall on the other side of the island, a wooden boardwalk is placed in the stream and the end was small brick tower, called Terrapin Tower. One can climb up and enjoy a complete overview of the whole natural spectacle from there. Afterwards, we walked on to Goat Island, which is covered with a variety of trees and spans an area of seventy acres. It looked to me, however, somewhat rugged and neglected. At the far end, one enjoys a spectacular view of the Niagara, which still rolls on undivided and, because of the slope of her channel, appears to be at a much higher level than the island. Nearby are also the Three Sisters, small tree-rich islands, among which the water forcefully carves.

Maid of the Mist, 1859

After we had seen the falls from all sides, there still remained an intriguing trip, namely to sail with a little steamboat, Maid of The Mist, underneath the bottom of the cataracts. This little vessel, exclusively built for this purpose, lies on the American side and makes the same trip every hour. As soon as one is on board, the ladies as

25

well as the gentlemen are draped with an oilskin coat, fitted with a hood. One wraps oneself as much as possible and takes a place on deck near the engine. The helmsman stands in a covered cabin; the steam whistle goes and the ship pushes off. One firstly sails straight towards the American Falls and as closely as possible alongside the foot. The engine labours against the oncoming stream. The same happens a little further down near the Canadian Falls, but here it stays at a respectful distance from the foot. The little boat sways and flies like an arrow over the waves back to the landing place. Everything is finished in a short half-hour. When nears the falls, the first sensation is anxiousness but one is so struck in the face with the plunging-down water that during the rocking of the ship and with the strong air suction, it becomes difficult to keep looking at the scene. It is like getting doused in the face with buckets of water. I would nevertheless encourage every visitor to the Niagara not to let this pass.

With this, I will end my description of the so very famous waterfalls. I could mention many legends and horrifying stories about this place but I will only say a few words about two of them. Tradition has it that the early inhabitants of this region, the Seneca Indians, made a human sacrifice every year to the spirit of the falls. For this purpose, a white canoe was loaded with flowers and fruits and then the prettiest girl of the tribe was put in and had to steer the little boat over the fall. It was an honour to be chosen and the unfortunate victim, under shouts of joy from the surrounding crowd, certainly met her end. Another heartbreaking event took place here just 10 years ago. An American family from Buffalo had visited the falls and returned happily from Goat Island, when one of the young men, laughing and joking, lifted up one of the girls of the party, and while saying, "I shall throw you in the water", held her above the water. From shock, the girl made a sudden move and fell out of his arms into the wild stream. The desperate young man fell and jumped in after her, and before the parents could cry out, both had fallen over the rocks down into the abyss. The corpse of the girl was discovered a few hours later between the rocks and the mutilated body of the young man was dredged up from the Niagara a few days after that.

The surroundings of the Niagara contain many important sites. I shall guide the readers to some of them. In the company of two

Englishmen, we visited our earlier travelling companions from the Asia,[44] and whom we had met again in an Indian village that is located a long hour's drive from the waterfalls. On Sunday, we found the Indians, who had all become Christians, gathered in their little wooden church. An American clergyman stood on a podium, and read English scriptures out of a Bible. Beside him stood an Indian who translated immediately for the congregation. He spoke quickly, but monotonously and very much through the nose. It was as if he uttered very short syllables. We found it rather important to be able to hear the Indian language, even if it did not sound harmonious or pleasant. He also did not know how to captivate his congregation because most of them were sleeping. Shortly afterward, the church service was over. The Indians with yellow skin and with long black hair wore European clothes and the women wore blue linen trousers, trimmed at the bottom with colours, with their heads wrapped in big blue veils. Their number is a good 500. They have their own chief and the state of New York has assigned them a defined, sizeable territory. They appeared to us still savage and unfriendly. Their village consists of scattered wooden huts, which do not look tidy."

Chapter Six
Returning to Niagara, 1859

Willem T. Gevers-Deynoot

"Returning to the village of Niagara, we noticed on the other side of the river of the same name, the monument of the English General [Sir Isaac Brock], a column 185 feet high, on the top of which his statue is placed. This monument was erected in 1853, after it was maliciously destroyed. General Brock lost his life for his fatherland in this area on October 13, 1812. Even more curious than the monument was the panorama that we enjoyed from the road. It is one of the expansive, spectacular scenes that make a visit to America so important. At a glance, one takes in an almost immeasurable forested area; the Niagara flows down below, a picture completed by the glittering Lake Ontario in the background.

While on the road, we also visited the so-called Devil's Hole, a deep foundering rock formation on the bank of the Niagara, especially noteworthy because of the terrible murder perpetrated here by Indians upon English soldiers who, without suspicion, set out near there and were all thrown in the abyss.

Another very important point is the suspension bridge, which is built two miles below the waterfalls over the Niagara River and connects the United States with Canada. The bridge is one of the nicest and most ingenious works that I have ever seen. Started in 1852, it was completed in 1855 and must have cost more than 500,000 dollars. The length amounts to 800 feet; the width is twenty-four feet and she is raised 250 feet above the Niagara. The bridge hangs on four iron cables, secured on both sides in the rocks, which are stretched over the brick towers of about 80 or 90 feet high. She has two level crossings above each other. The top one is used for steam trains, the lower for other carriages and pedestrians. The bridge combines speed and power and I repeatedly saw steam trains going over at half-speed, without it bending. The bridge is safeguarded against swinging with a number of stabilizing wires on both sides.

Suspension Bridge, Niagara Falls, 1860

Looking on in amazement about this masterpiece of human labour, however, still more striking is the landscape that nature provides here. A lovelier place, I can hardly remember. The clear blue Niagara flows down below between upright walls of red sandstone, which are abundantly overgrown with greenery, while the large waterfalls take shape in the distance. The various hues, the trees, the water — everything comes together to give this place a grand character. Still, it had been just two days before our arrival the scene of excessive human folly. It was here that Blondin had performed his so widely trumpeted act[45]. One still saw the platform, which had been constructed for that purpose, and traces of the crowds that had jostled each other.

I considered myself lucky not to have to seen this and I believe that a human being can better employ his audacity than dance the tightrope above a deep gulf.

Among the other points of interest near the Niagara, I still have to mention two: One, the burning well, and two, the belvedere on the battlefield of Lundy's Lane. The first is a well near the bank of the Niagara, located a few miles above the falls. The water is so much impregnated with inflammable gas that, with the slightest spark, a clear flame will erupt. I had seldom seen such a high concentration. It is worth a visit, if only for the splendid views of the river, which one enjoys while on the road toward it and also because of a most curious floating island, which one can walk over.

The belvedere is a wooden construction that is climbed by 134 steps. It is built where the battle took place between the English and Americans on July 25, 1814, each party claiming victory. In order to get a good view of the surrounding countryside, it is worth the climb.

The location of our hotel was, as I have already briefly mentioned, very practical for the visitor to this area and whatever the American travel books may say, I would advise to always first see the falls on the Canadian side. Besides that, Clifton House was an outstanding inn with two large galleries, from where we enjoyed a splendid view. The only unpleasant thing was that through the vibration of the air, due to the proximity to the falls, the doors and windows rattled continuously and when the wind blew towards the hotel, anyone in front of the door would be standing in mist. On the other hand, the evenings and nights were lovely, especially when I saw the terribly startling waters from my room during clear moonshine. The loud thunder was heard without a break; this has taken place for thousands of years, and will continue for thousands more.

Many families were quartered in our hotel. Niagara is a Mecca for the Americans. The ladies competed with each other by the diversity and richness of their gowns, and I found amongst the Americans much more refinement than in our hotels in the White Mountains. Amongst the guests was a prominent Belgian painter, who travelled here every year to make studies and it saddened me that no other European artists cross to North America to see the splendid nature scenes.

Finally, I will say something about a strange event that took place during our stay at Clifton House. On the American side of the waterfalls in one of the largest hotels, a family from New Orleans was quartered, accompanied by a stout twenty-three-year-old slave, to take care of the children. With her slave's heart, she knew, every way possible, probably by ferry, to get across the Niagara and applied as a maidservant at Clifton House. She was hired and started her work. A few hours later, the owner of the slave, who had noticed her absence and had searched for her, walked into our hotel. He asked for the runaway girl and persuaded the hotel owner to speak to her in a neighboring house, in his presence. The planter brought to his slave's attention the wrongful behaviour and tried with pleasant promises to persuade her to return with him to the other side of the Niagara, however, to no avail. The girl willfully refused to follow her master. Since she was on English territory, the use of physical violence was very risky, so the American finally decided to give up the case for the moment, but persuaded the innkeeper to keep her confined in the house until nightfall. In the meantime, the servants in Clifton House, almost all Negroes, among them also some runaway slaves, noticed what was going on. Barely had the planter left when they, knowing that the girl did not return to the hotel, put their heads together and demanded information about the case from the innkeeper. By his promises, he was bound to the owner and could not give them a sufficient answer. At the wink of an eye, all servants marched to the neighbouring house, which was locked. They knocked down the doors and freed the frightened girl. One of the Negroes undertook right away the task of taking her under his care, and helped her to get northward to Toronto.[46] The bird had flown. The planter could complain that he had lost one of his best girl slaves; but friends of humanity rejoiced."

Chapter Seven
Niagara–Toronto, 1888

Bernard C. Schuijlenburg

Bernard Christiaan Schuijlenburg

Lokaal „Odeon" Singel,
VRIJDAGAVOND 6 APRIL,
Reisvoordracht van den Heer
LISSONE,
naar **Londen** en de **Schotsche
Hooglanden,** aanschouwelijk
voorgesteld door den Heer MER-
KELBACH, met geheel nieuwe
lichtbeelden (dissolving views),
zoodat de bezoeker als het ware
de geheele intressante Reis mede
maakt.
Bezoek aan Buffalo Bills, Voor-
stelling te Londen; en na de
Schotsche Reis eenige belangrijke
Gezichtspunten der Reis Amerika
en Canada, welke in Mei a. s. zal
plaats hebben.
Aanvang 8 uur. Entrée f 1.—.
Bespreken 10 Cent extra, aan het
Lokaal en aan het Ned. Touristen-
Bureau, Singel 159. (5991)

Advertisement by Lissone, in *Het Nieuws van den Dag,* April 5, 1888

The journey along the Great Lakes continued as the visitors took their leave of spectacular Niagara, returning to Toronto. Bernard Christiaan Schuijlenburg, a captain intendant with the Koninklijk Nederlandsch-Indisch Leger (Royal Netherlands East Indies Army), chronicles this leg of the journey in a language replete with superlatives. He had been drawn to his trip by a mere newspaper advertisement[47], eventually signing up for an all-in tour through the United States and Canada. The tour was that was taking place the coming May, was organized by Lissone from Amsterdam, an enterprise that eventually became The Netherland's first and most renowned travel agency, named for its founder Jac. P. Lissone[48]. It took place in the company of a group of six compatriots, two women and four men, one of whom was the male tour guide. Unfortunately, Schuijlenburg does not disclose the names of his travel mates. After having seen the Falls, the group continued their journey through Canada towards Montreal by boarding a ship at Youngstown, N.Y. (located near Fort Niagara) that would take them across Lake Ontario to Toronto.

"After several more passengers have come on board, we steam up the very calm Lake Ontario. Notwithstanding that it is known as the

smallest and certainly the narrowest of the five large lakes, still this one is so wide that we cannot see the opposite side. We are soon on the open sea, so to speak, and see during a short half-hour nothing other than the silver water and the azure blue sky with a small boat and a few plumes of smoke in the background to prove that we are not drifting around abandoned before we see the Canadian coast loom ahead on the horizon. Yet, we soon near it. Against the more or less hilly beach, we can soon distinguish a few spires and large buildings and, within a short time, we see the small town of Toronto as a panorama stretched out in front of us. Our steamer worked its way skillfully amongst several small yachts, small freighters and small pleasure boats. It suddenly scooted between two landing stages, and after adjusting by a few strokes backwards, it came to a halt and gave us the opportunity to disembark.

On board, we had deliberated about whether we would travel by rail or by boat from Toronto to Kingston, the entrance of the St. Lawrence with the Thousand Islands, the actual objective of our journey. With the first-mentioned means of transport, we could stay the whole day in Toronto so as to depart at twelve o'clock at night and to sit in the train until five o'clock in the morning. With the steamer, we had to depart at 3 o'clock and we had to stay all day and night on board. We chose, however, the last option, because Toronto was not interesting enough to stay there any longer than a few hours. We would not have a decent night's sleep if we would travel on by rail, while the boat promised us, especially with the beautiful summer weather, a lovely trip and a calm night and still permitted us to see the city with a glance.

We went immediately on our way and arrived (after having meandered through a lot of commotion from freight trains and warehouses) at the beautiful Yonge Street, which we walked on until we stopped at the corner of Front Street to view the magnificent building of the Bank of Montreal. At Adelaide Street, we discovered the large and spacious, yet also decorative, post office that excelled in its sound and practical layout. At Church Street, we saw the Normal School, a lovely small mansion, where the province's teaching staff is educated and formed and, by Carlton Street, we turned left to reach Queen's Park.

There we sat down for a moment under the lovely foliage of the decorative shade trees grouped between the shrubs. We made a short walk around the Toronto University that is erected in strict Normandy style, with a front of 300 feet and a depth of 250 feet. Its wide blunt tower on the right is considered the nicest building in the city; and we viewed the bronze statue of Queen Victoria, bordering the elegant column in remembrance of the Canadian volunteers who defended the borders in June 1866 against the Fenians.[49]

Further, we walked back again along the wide and beautiful College Avenue and reached Queen Street, the alluring Osgoode Hall, the sanctuary of justice, where we rested a moment, afterwards to go through Spadina Street into King Street, the cozy and busy artery of this small trading town that, by the way, already counts for more than 150,000 residents.

The lively bustle of trams and trucks, of carriages and pedestrians did not prevent a parade from passing in this main street (which is shaped by high buildings and where mostly beautifully displayed shops and stores are established) which was comprised out of a music band, followed by eight strangely dressed-up gentlemen who led five ladies in the midst of them. To my question as to what this all meant, the answer was that this was a promotion display of thirteen artists of a comedy troupe, which would perform a tragedy tonight. For that matter, programs were dealt out from all sides with a lavish hand and put in the pedestrians' pockets.

Alongside the uninteresting Government House, from where the government rules the province, we reached Rossin House,[50] *the best hotel of town, where an excellent lunch arranged by Lissone awaited us.*[51]

After our long walk, it was very welcome and that is why we gave it due attention, which the beautifully prepared meals fully deserved.

And during the fine dessert, when we had drunk a small glass of English ale of excellent quality, it was time to go again to the harbour which, this time, we reached through York and Front Street and past the custom house."

Rossin House Hotel (flying flag), King and York, Toronto 1885–1895

Chapter Eight

Toronto to Kingston, 1888

Bernard C. Schuijlenburg

To continue the tour going toward Montreal, travellers had to board another boat. The next port of call after Toronto was the town of Kingston. Schuijlenburg and his party of fellow travellers also took this route.

"The civil servants at customs have not made it at all difficult for us and, without having to open our suitcases, we can take them into Canadian territory and board the steamer Spartan that soon cleaves through the calm lake.

The *Spartan* leaving Alexandria Bay, 1890

We shall have to spend about thirty hours on this vessel; cabins are allocated to us which are not at all roomy and airy. The ladies are so lucky to get a separate room; the four gentlemen have to share a small cabin with four bunks and Lissone [the tour guide] ends up somewhere with a small group of queer customers in a large cabin.

One would be very mistaken if one, in respect to our steamship, wanted to conclude that all luxury is banned and that one lives there in Spartan simplicity. The opposite is true, because the salons excel in luxury and tidiness and the meals excel by abundance and good flavour. And our vessel sails fast because the pleasant clapping of the paddles takes us with great speed onto the calm lake, now towards a few ships, then passing small sailboats and small steamships and leaving them behind.

The coast is more or less mountainous or, better said, set with surprisingly high dunes. We remain continuously within sight of Canada, so that we get to see nothing of the American territory.

Close to four o'clock, we again set course for the shore to moor near Scarborough Junction, an important station of the Grand Trunk Railway, where we take on great number of passengers.

At 5:30, we dash past the jetty of Whitby, where we only stop for a short time, and at 7:30, we put into the tidy little harbour of Port Hope. A cozy bustle prevails there, hundreds of ladies and gentlemen had planned their evening walk in such a way that they could see the steamer dock, strolling back and forth on the jetty, happily chatting and waving at the passengers with handkerchiefs and bouquets, with which the delightful sex were amply provided. Several small longboats of all shapes, long booms, small boats, jolly boats, canoes and even watershoes and pedal boats floated around us with a hustle and bustle, like ants around their destroyed nest. In rowing fast and skillful steering, it seemed that the ladies here were on equal terms with the gents.

It was already dark when we arrived in Coburg so we did not get to see much of it, even less because, at least to me, the beauty of the star-spangled sky had this time not that much influence so that I was able to resist the touch of Morpheus. When I, at any rate, was awakened at eleven o'clock because of the nightly chill, I noticed that I had already been sleeping for several hours in one of the most comfortable chairs on deck. Because my travel pals had also already disappeared, there was nothing better to do than to carry on that important activity in my cabin.

However at 5:30 in the morning of Wednesday July 4, I am again present to watch the ships sailing in and out of Kingston."

Kingston, 1825

Duke Bernhard of Saxe-Weimar-Eisenach

The visit to Kingston at the end of the 19th century by Schuijlenburg was an uneventful affair for the city. This was in great contrast to the experience of Duke of Saxe-Weimar-Eisenach whose arrival in Kingston was reported in the *Kingston Chronicle*.[52] The Duke, travelling through Canada in 1825 with his entourage[53], was officially welcomed with an honour guard. Duke Bernhard, being a military man, keen observer and articulate reporter provided his views of international political affairs of the time, specifically a breach of naval military law.

Duke Bernhard of Saxe-Weimar-Eisenach

"*Toward nine in the evening, we arrived in Kingston, the British naval harbour on Lake Ontario, located on a bay. We dropped anchor near the city; I remained aboard ship for the night. When I awoke the following morning, I found a company of the 37th Regiment, which is garrisoned here, along with its band, formed in line on the quay near the ship as an honour guard. I dismissed them immediately, of course. After receiving several of the officers, we sailed across the bay to the dockyard — built across from Kingston, surrounded by a high wall and manned by a strong watch. I discovered from the navy-list that there are ten ships with 306 guns ordinarily stationed here. It appeared to me that in this instance they listed the number of pieces too low. The St. Lawrence, one of these vessels, carries 120 pieces, while two ships still on the slipway, the Montreal and the Wolf, are three-deckers equipped to carry 130 pieces each, but which appear on the list as smaller. Following the Treaty of Ghent [Rush-Bagot Agreement], it is no longer permitted to construct any new vessels during peacetime; the arsenal staff, therefore, aside from the necessary officers and officials, consists of only twelve carpenters who have little else to occupy them than working on a small and very elegantly-built schooner, which is to be launched soon and is to serve as a yacht. The largest of the vessels on the slipway is uncovered and seems to have suffered greatly from the weather. The St. Lawrence is the largest ship afloat but is also in a dilapidated condition, especially below the waterline, where the ship suffers from the freshwater and is being eaten away by worms. The dockyard quay is constructed of wood and bears the impression of the haste with which it was constructed; it is in a bad state of repair. Several years ago, they had built a 192-foot-long sandstone storehouse, three stories high and with iron doors and shutters, for the storage of sails and rope. The inside partitions are made of wood. Directly after our entering the storehouse, the iron entrance doors were closed and remained closed, for they express a great distrust of the Americans here. Below the building is a cellar, also set up as a storehouse, the floor of which is limestone and serves the entire building as a foundation. The stairs in the building are of stone and built inside a stone tower; they intend, in time, to also make the floors of the various levels of iron, thus rendering the storehouse fireproof, much like a similar one in Plymouth. The smithy is located in a special massive building, while* the offices are in a third. Adjacent to the offices is a large hall, on the floor of which are drawn the various measurements for the ships to be built. Across from the dockyard, which has been built on a promontory, is yet another promontory, Fort Frederick, which I did not have the time, however, to visit. On an elevation behind the dockyard were a number of tents. We discovered that there were about four hundred Irish emigrants camped here, whom the British government had transported from their native country at its own expense to clear the northwest shore of Lake Ontario. They will soon be leaving here. The city of Kingston has some two thousand residents, and, with respect to its construction, is not particularly noteworthy.

We departed Kingston after eleven o'clock aboard the steamship Lady Dalhousie, which will take us to Prescott, sixty-eight miles from Kingston, on the left bank of the St. Lawrence. Our company remained the same, except that adjutant Maitland had left us in Kingston."

Chapter Nine
Kingston Through Thousand Islands, 1888

Bernard C. Schuijlenburg

"At 5:30 in the morning of Wednesday July 4, I am however, again present to watch the ships sailing in and out of Kingston. There, we get fifty more passengers on board, who had departed by the night train from Toronto and at present, apparently in order to freshen up, may wait for half an hour on the pier for the Spartan. We do not have to fear for a shortage of space, because the vessels of the Richelieu & Ontario Navigation Company are roomy and comfortably furnished. The passengers, for the most part tourists, all easily found a seat or chosen a promenade place before the prow turned into the St. Lawrence.

We can now take advantage of the general procedure created by the Rome, Watertown & Ogdensburg Railroad Co., in conjunction with the before-mentioned steamship company. It requires that every passenger be given a large book with a couple of hundred pages as a present, containing an excellent description of the planned trip. All of this is explained and garnished with a few hundred neat and lovely drawings and sketches, and with various comprehensive and accurate charts and maps. In no library would its beauty be misplaced. It is handy and helped us when we looked for names and explanations of the various beautiful spots which we passed in succession.

It is still fresh on deck as we cross over from Kingston to Cape Vincent, which is about eleven miles away in New York state; but the beautiful weather that has soon removed all clouds and morning haze and has painted the sky with gorgeous azure gives the summer sun the opportunity to beam its basking rays upon us. And when we also sail into the actual river, then it is already in every way a joy to sit and walk above on deck and to breathe the cool and healthy air there, which is being brought to us by a light breeze over the enchanting group of islands and which charge it with the loveliest smells of forests and flowers. Because we do not desire to enter the giant stream before we have already found our safe way through the maze of small islands of lovely over-grown rocks, and also of green reefs rising just a bit above the water, divided by deep and narrow gorges, by deceptive channels and unreliable waters, and which are generally known by the name 'Thousand Islands'.

In fact, according to my guidebook, there are more than 1,800 of these lovely emeralds and glittering precious stones, which seemed to have raised themselves out of the deep crystal clear water, to be admired by the people, and are in many variations from the smallest rock points, and like a basket of beautiful flowers and lovely green, keep floating above the water level, up to the picturesque islands, miles across and covered with the richest and most luxuriant plant growth. In the last years, a large number of the beautiful, floating gardens and parks were bought by private persons who have built elegant villas and expensive summer cottages which, along with the beautiful hotels on Cape Vincent, Clayton, Round Island Park, Westminster Park and Alexandria Bay, have contributed their gifts to transform this area into one of the most visited 'pleasure resorts' of America, in one of the loveliest idyllic spots of the whole world.

During the mild season, the lovely islands create cheerfulness and liveliness, and the countless channels and coves of the St. Lawrence are then dotted with small sailing yachts and pleasure boats which glide around the lovely bits of land like gondolas between the Venetian palaces erected out of wet elements. And that pleasurable scene of tireless activity, of liveliness and cheerfulness started when the sun showed on the horizon and continued until the shadows of the lovely tree groups got longer and the western horizon colours with a lovely red sunset that makes the green spots look even nicer. If that also threatens to be replaced by nightly darkness, then one sees one after the other villa or country house lighting their many multicoloured lights.

One then sees the small yachts with their slim masts, and rangy yards and gaffs as a friendly answer decorated with rows of lanterns, until an illumination starts, so neat and rich, that it seems to compete with that of Venice when it is decorated with the abundant lighting in the carnival period.

It was a beautiful sailing, a trip of peaceful enjoyment, near a series of splendid nature scenes, all just as fascinating as lovely. Moreover, there was something festive about the area — after all, no house was too small, no villa too large, no castle too glorious for the flag of the United States to flutter gaily from a high pole in honour of Independence Day, which is being celebrated. The Yankees love flags and ribbons. If they can somehow find a motive to put them out, they gladly seize the opportunity, so one can imagine that the favourite colours would never be missing. Even the English, although their tastes mostly differ from that of the common man, seem to recognize this and also hoisted bunting on their fancy residences.

At one of the small islands, people were busy putting the final touch on a residence, or let me rather say, on a luxurious palace that was built by the New Yorker, Vanderbilt, in order to spend ten days there every summer. It looked beautiful and in the small harbour (that the big railway king had delved) already moored a neatly rigged small cutter and a small steam yacht that excelled in smartness and style. From a discourse that two Americans held in my proximity, I heard that the big capitalist built it for the trifling sum of two million dollars.

A feverish activity prevails now and then at the landing places where we are moored now and then. Not from loading and unloading of commercial goods, not trading activity, not a rush of lorries and tow carts, but from a pleasing bustle of cheerful passengers and tourists, of clubs who go for a picnic, of ladies and gentlemen who are going fishing, of sportsmen who will measure each others' strength in rowing and each others' skillfulness in sailing. It is an Eldorado for all these amusements here, especially for lovers of angling because a river rich with fish seems to be hard to find. In particular, large salmon will be found in the numerous rapids, which make navigating on the St. Lawrence so very difficult and even dangerous at some points.

Here and there however, the wide stream narrows while it gets shallower since rock bands and reefs, as it were, have formed in-between and over which the water throws itself with wild force in large foaming waves, and fierce turning whirlpools point out the places where the surf is strongest and the danger is greatest. For many years the river was, for that reason, declared unsuitable for shipping, until finally the Indian pilot Teronhiahere became known. He had drifted hundred times down the stream with his canoe and knew the waterway like the back of his hand. He also knew how to map it and to the great surprise of the public was able to safely navigate a steamship from Kingston to Montreal. After that, the ice was broken, except that even the most powerful steamers could not return — they were unable to work their way back up against the ferocious stream.

Yet, that was not the end of it, because it was decided to dig channels, in such a way, so that the ships destined upstream could navigate it a bit below the rapids, so as to enter again the great waterway above the rapids. In this way, they have been able to cut off the Galop, du Plat, Long Sault, Coteau, Cedar, Split Rock, Cascades and Lachine Rapids with a variety of more or less costly waterworks. One of which, the Beauharnois Canal, certainly takes a first place. The river widens here and there until such a width, that one has given at some parts, not inaccurately or without cause, the name 'lake'. So, for example, the 25-miles-long stretch between Long Sault and Coteau Rapids is called 'Lake St. Francis' and that between the Cascades and Lachine Rapids is 'Lake St. Louis'.

When we cut through the waves of the calm last mentioned, it is not without suspense that we see in the distance the outlet being obstructed by a long wide line of white foam, here and there interrupted by a black stone mass or by a rock on which a most luxuriant vegetation had nestled. Yet the ship's crew is ready for its task and, pondering the results from the surveys of another famous Indian pilot, Baptiste, the course is set for a place where the water curls up and seethes, where the wild crests of the rolling waves dissolve into a series of splashes and white flocks, which is eagerly seized by clear sunlight to conjure up the most beautiful medley of colours. We soar forward; in that way we are swept away by the stream until we suddenly get a jolt, so severe that some tabourets roll over and most of the passengers grasped the rigging, railings, etc.

It signals that we have entered the Lachine Rapids and that we have steamed into the ferocious stream, where no power in the world could make us turn around to go back. The Spartan is now and then jerked and swayed, like a vessel on a high difficult sea. The nose of the ship pitches downward and the stern sticks out completely above the water; every time we get a 'small sea', over the front deck. On the left, rocks; at starboard, cliffs; straight in front, a few islands; and continuously, we speed forward seemingly headed for certain disaster, fed not only by the stream, but also by our engine that remains on full power, 'forward'. Yet, at a certain moment, we see a narrow channel to which the bowsprit soon points the route. We fly into there with a masterly turn, not a metre off the correct course, for if we would have come a fathom more to the left, then our funnel would be smashed against overhanging and waving tree limbs, while a few feet more to the right, the starboard paddle was threatened with certain destruction by a large rock.

Exciting moments are, however, soon over and we have also this danger behind us. Yet these rapids are not always so easy to pass and when a storm howls, or only a strong southern wind blows, then the pilot does not always so confidently enter the maze of small natural channels and treacherous gullies, and he prefers to also use the completely safe, but rather expensively delved channel downstream. During heavy rains, in fog or after sundown, the latter is always used. When one cannot read the small signs of the eddy currents and whirlpools, then even the most competent pilot does not dare to take on the journey.

Soon we will have Nuns' Island (Ile des Soeurs) in sight which was earlier used by the Indians as a cemetery for the heroes that fell in battle against enemy tribes. But it is now in possession of a monastery in Montreal, part of which was made into a park. On our right hand, we pass by and leave behind a few light ships and soon the world-famous Victoria Bridge looms in front of us, the large railway connection between the mainland and Montreal. She is supposed to be the longest bridge in the world and measures almost 10,000 feet, of which more than 1¼ English miles hangs above the water at such a height that we can sail underneath it with great ease. She is made up of a regular iron tunnel, completely covered and walled, because

Congregation of Notre Dame, Nuns' Island, about 1900

during the rough winter season, such strong storms sometimes prevail that a train could easily derail and could blow into the stream. The bridge also rests, not only on the two heavy land abutments, but also on twenty-four massive brick pillars, which, because of the floating ice, have sharp granite edges on the streaming side. She cost no less than 6½ million dollars or 16 million guilders. For America, it took a surprisingly long time to build, five years. In 1860, when he made his well-known trip through the New World, the Prince of Wales officially opened it for public traffic.

Soon we are in sight of the spires and high buildings of Montreal. The panorama of the city is additionally enhanced by the high rigging of the various sea-going vessels. It is lovely to sail into, especially because the background is formed by a few high hills which are lushly overgrown and where the many domed roofs show up in a lovely way, as if they were being polished by the evening sun. And soon, we are in front of the city that is built on the St. Lawrence, in the same way as Antwerp on the Schelde. Colossal vessels and steamboats are anchored on the river or moored at the spacious quays. Beautifully carved and slim-line rigged mail steamers are disgorging thick smoke clouds, busily loading and unloading with great buzz.

Montreal is an English possession, however the trade seems to be for the most part maintained with France. At any rate, the tricolour of that state proved to have the upper hand over the flags of other nations. Amongst the luxury passenger ships, we noticed a few which maintained a scheduled service with Le Havre. Some other steamers also carried, besides their own name, the name of the city 'Bordeaux', proof that they also belong to the country of wine. For that matter, it is the reason that Montreal has so many connections with France. Remember that the Frenchman, Jacques Cartier established the city 300 years ago. In the later centuries a tremendous number of his countrymen have settled there, and that, for relatively short time, has been transferred to in the hands of the English, who, so far, have not succeeded in imposing the English national character upon the city.

We sail towards the shore and halt near a large riversteamship, the Quebec, which maintains the link with the city of that name. A large number of the passengers transfer onto it, while the moving of the luggage and the cargo gives us a fifteen-minute opportunity to size up the roadstead and the surrounding area. It is spacious and provides a vast area for shipping, better understood when I explain that the city is located on a small island that is surrounded on all sides by deep water. Although being 800 miles from the ocean, the largest seagoing ships can anchor anywhere.

Soon we steam again and after a few minutes sailing, we dart into a lock of the Lachine Canal. While the Spartan is immediately prepared for its return trip the next morning, we leave it behind to take a seat in an omnibus that will soon take us city-bound. Via McGill Street, we reach Victoria Square. Then we turn right into St. James Street to stop shortly afterward in front of our hotel, the splendid St. Lawrence Hall, the city's best hotel. It looks tidy there and everything is fixed up according the American system — clean saloons, good airy rooms and, last but not least, an excellent supper awaited us there. After we had given due attention to the latter, some of us still wished to go for a stroll, and the Lissone guide and I went to check into what the mail may have delivered to us."

St. Lawrence Hall, Montreal, about 1890

Chapter Ten

Montreal, 1888

Bernard C. Schuijlenburg

"For it, we truly do not have to walk too far, because the large and well-furnished Post Office is not even ten houses from us, so we are soon in possession of our letters and newspapers. The streets are enjoyably busy and pleasantly lit. It is notable that one sees so many French names everywhere, on stores as well as on public roads and squares, while one also hears at least as much French as English spoken. We walk on until the Place d'Armes at Champ de Mars, turn right into St. Gabriel Street, so as to soon arrive at Notre Dame Street, which we walk through until it is called St. Joseph Street, and by Inspector and St. Bonaventure streets we reach again St. James Street and our hotel.

The stores seemed to be open longer than in the United States and also the cafés here have the more enjoyable French character. It does not have to be said once we popped inside and soon had a tasty mug of foaming Cambrinus [beer] in front of us that tasted delicious along with the beautiful summer weather which we were enjoying while seated beneath a pergola. And soon I bought one of the just-issued evening papers from a newspaper-boy to look at something I was somewhat curious about, namely how Mr. Flack[54] had fared in the Niagara. The article, "Died in the Rapids", confirmed immediately the general opinion, that this reckless man also would taste defeat. For the sake of curiosity, I copy the following from it:

By the time he passed under the Cantilever bridge, the craft was in the centre of the river in the swift current and moved faster and faster, Flack throwing kisses to the spectators. When it reached the railway suspension bridge, it darted under it like an arrow from a bow, Flack doing his utmost to steer towards the Canadian side and when it reached the first rapids, one struck it broadside and turned it in a complete somersault, after which she righted herself. Flack was seen working the paddles and the little craft soon righted herself and rode the other large rapids gracefully until it reached the Whirlpool Rapids, where the water rolls mountains high in its madness to force itself down through the narrow channel. A large wave struck and swelled over the boat, completely submerging it and its occupant for fully thirty seconds. When she emerged from the breaker, Flack was seen to shake his head and wave both his hands.

The craft then rode all right until it reached the maelstrom of the Whirlpool, at the place known as Capt. Webb's Point, named after him as the place where he was last seen in making his fatal swim of the rapids on the 24th July, 1883. At this point the same fate met Flack. His little boat was struck broadside by a large break and turned upside down, and remained that way sailing into the Whirlpool, and undoubtedly Flack was unable to right it, and the weight of his body keeping in that position, drowned him. The excitement was intense, people running towards the Whirlpool, there being numbers of excursionists present. The little craft made five trips around the pool, upside-down, it taking about one hour for her to make these circles...

When the boat was towed to the shore and was turned over, there was Flack dead, and the pin in the buckle of the *belt out. Undoubtedly Flack, seeing he was unable to right the boat, attempted to extricate himself from the fastenings and failed. His body was brought up to the top of the riverbank and up to the bridge, bearing no mark of any description on it. His sister and brother-in-law, Mr. and Mrs. Stephenson, and his sixteen-year-old son, were present and witnessed the whole trip. Flack has a wife and five young children at Syracuse.*

Yet enough! I leave it to everyone to reflect about the character of the family Flack and about the emotions under which the poor widow will have spent the last day. I proclaimed to my companion the theory that such recklessness must be forbidden by the governments and that everyone who tried to undertake such activities could be brought to other thoughts by 50 lashes at his behind. And while discussing this, we went to our rooms, where all memories about the drama were soon forgotten in sleep.

At 7:30 in the morning of Thursday July 5, our complete party was together at breakfast, after which we went on our way through St. James and Francois Xavier streets to the cathedral Notre Dame located three minutes away. It is a splendid building which is built in the same style as its namesake in Paris and with both of its front-placed towers of 227 feet, it makes an impressive effect. The inside measurements are extremely large — the length amounts to no less than 220 feet, the height almost 80 feet and the width 120 feet, so that when large number of visitors for general events are anticipated, there are about 15,000 seats. In one of the towers hangs the well-known Gross Bourdon, one of the largest bells in the world, which is six feet high and 8½ feet wide, while she weighs nearly 25,000 English pounds.

We were particularly lucky because, just as we entered, a funeral service commenced for someone who apparently had a large fortune at his disposal during his lifetime. At least, no cost was spared to give the church a solemn appearance. There is so much crepe and the like applied that even a part of the beautiful paintings and its masterly turned-out plasterwork is covered and thus snatched from the eye. And then the devout priests gathered (followed by a host of choirboys, all just as richly and imposingly dressed) and voiced the solemn prayer *songs to Heaven accompanied by the heavy organ music and slowly withdrawing into the rooms beside the beautiful altar while hundreds of lofty wax candles successively disappear in front of our eyes. Suddenly, a contrast so sharp and offensive follows that all sobriety by the audience had to disappear.*

After all, the clergy had hardly left the coffin placed on the platform in the centre of the church surrounded by a number of candles, crosses and statues when a bunch of labourers dressed in their customary workmen's outfit swooped upon it. Talking and laughing, they carry away all the ceremonial artifacts used. Rather rudely, the shroud is pulled away and while poking fun, the whole platform (on which only an imitation coffin was placed, so that there could, of course, be not a bit of a real corpse) is dismantled and stored until the next occasion. And I, who in my innocent ignorance, was under the impression that one would soon proceed with a funeral, had to hear that the devoted, for which the service was held, had passed away no less than 27 years ago, and long since "unto dust have returned".

While returning to our hotel, we stopped for a moment in front of a group of three buildings, which in all aspects are worthy of a closer view. They are namely the Post Office, the Bank of Montreal, and the head offices of the Canadian Pacific Railway. The first is constructed out of grey stones in a modern Italian style and has a beautiful front decorated with fine pillars that is crowned with a wide-domed tower, in which the extremely large dials of the city clock make the hour known to the whole town. The second has a portico, which is carried by eight high columns and gives entrance to the inside through a beautiful gate, while the third is constructed in very decorative architectural style, which is unknown to me.

We found our smart clean landau already waiting for us, so that we were very soon on our way to see the most interesting item in the city. Our first visit was Nelson's monument in Notre Dame Street, where a nicely sculptured square plinth carries a high round pillar on which a large statue of the hero is placed. Afterward, in the same street, we arrive at the large Court House, a piece of art in Greek architectural style, with a front of about 300 feet that is almost completely covered by a colossal Ionian portico, which is not in danger of monotony because of three entrances equipped with protruding stairways. And as if it were complementary, there is City Hall, constructed in modern French style, with its 485-foot-long front and its nicely finished towers, a true jewel of the city.

Now we turn right and come through St. Jacques Cartier square, where in memory to Sebastopol, two large Russian cannons lay rusting at the Bon Secours Market, an extremely large building which, with its frontage of more than 500 feet, covers the landing stage of a number of small steamships. A few days each week, the most important market of the whole of Canada is held there, and it must also be a very interesting scene to see the mishmash of curious traditional costumes together and to hear the many various English, Irish, Scottish, Breton and Southern French accents and dialects.

Now we reach the Champs de Mars, a large park which is worthwhile visiting, more for its historic memories than for its nice layout. According to the stories, in all America there should be found no other piece of ground where so many armies from so many different nations, in the most varied military dress, have been inspected as on this terrain. Yet, about that, we see nothing anymore. We soon drive into St. Dennis Street, passing the lovely Trinity Church towards the Notre Dame de Lourdes, a newly opened church that we will visit. She is not big, but clean and tastefully furnished. The intriguing part about it is the dark niche where the lovely figure of the patroness is placed. One has been able to catch the heavenly light in such a way and filter it through strange coloured glasses, that everything seems to be shrouded in secrecy, and in every way suitable to make vivid impressions on simple and superstitious people.

Soon we drive further and pass the notably large hospital, Hôtel Dieu, where there is room for several hundred patients and which commands attention in all aspects, because of the large park where it is being built, as well as by the high, gilded, iron-domed tower, with which it is crowned. In the meantime, we near Mount Royal, the high hill from where the city derives its name and which still exists there in all its natural beauty, in its magnificent decorations of primeval forest and foliage, where, as yet, only a few roads and footpaths have taken away a part of the original character.

Against the foot on the east side, we find the Cemetery, where a few beautifully laid-out lanes slowly meander upwards, every now and then intersecting wide paths which lead to the beautifully foliaged spots where the dead have found their resting places. The layout is particularly grand and skillful; the available space is vast, with wonderful tombstones surrounded with a splendour of flowers, decorative monuments, half-concealed under softly rustling weeping willows and lilacs hanging downwards. Revealing monuments from which the profound grief of those left behind speak so touchingly. They lay here so still, so peacefully together in this quiet area. In such endearing surroundings, the ever-frightening picture of death is suppressed by the solemn feeling of thankfulness towards the Creator.

While reading the names of the dead, we feel our attention distracted by the soft rustling of a brook caused by the splashing water of a clean, small, water fountain. We stop our discourse to listen to the lovely chirping of the birds, whose tone is soon drowned out by the solemn song of the lark who, light up, almost invisible to the human eye, acclaims with a loud voice the wonderfully impressive nature of this lovely place. Then it is only necessary that we leave this solemn cemetery to get higher up on Mount Royal. As yet, the words of the psalmist: "Quiet rest place of God's dead, I think about you with sweet joy", at least not for this cemetery or nor for the Brooklyn Greenwood Cemetery, will soon leave my memory.

In between the Ur-trees, heavy trunks, low brushwood and through thickly twining plants, the road winds constantly upwards until we finally reach a sort of plateau, where the coachmen asks us to step out. And when we have walked to a wide platform, there awaits for us an overwhelmingly nice surprise. After all, we are at the top of Mount Royal which, at any rate the upper part, crumbled off rather steeply and well onto the side facing the city. The view is not blocked by anything and a gorgeous panorama stretches out at our feet.

The city is close below us with her gathering spires and domed roofs, her large buildings, her green parks, her wide streets and spacious gardens in the sunlight. Right and left from there are lovely forests and small hills, and behind all that, like a huge silver ribbon, is the beautiful St. Lawrence River, where large ocean steamers and sailing ships are calmly swaying, while the riverboats and smaller vessels provide a pleasant activity to the water. Far away in the distance, we see the large Victoria Bridge and behind it, now hardly noticeable, a white-shining strip, from which we recognize the Lachine Rapids. At the other side are the Vermont Mountains close to the horizon, leaving for our eyes an open prosperous area, where large farms and properties full of many coloured crops divided by small strips of forest, form a most pleasant pattern.

And in our vicinity is the Ur-forest with its majestic oaks, its huge pine trees trunks and its shady rich foliage. All this makes a beautiful view, an indescribably lovely scene.

I should not have to mention that a few fellows have nestled here with telescopes through which one, for a few cents, can take a glance, that a few men in a friendly manner invited us to hear their explanation about some points that all are of particular interest, and that three small stands are erected, where one can get all kinds of souvenirs, like photographs, etc. And neither do I also have to mention that we, of course, did not let our legs be pulled by this horde of swindlers but rather used the information which was given to us by our very benevolent coachman.

After having a half-hour repose here and enjoying to our heart's content this wonderful scene, we returned this time via a steep, but also much shorter route, that took us past a point also providing a very nice view and which is accessible by a high tobogganing tramway through which the pedestrians are spared the tiresome journey to the highest point. We pass a nice fountain, which is also a watering place for our horses, and soon arrive again in the city, at about the height of the large park, in the centre of which the colossal McGill College is built.

Turning left, we arrive in Sherbrooke Street, the wide lane planted with leafy trees, along which the luxurious houses, the beautiful villas and expensive palaces of the haute volée form rows of luxury. According to our guidebooks, this street is surpassed in beauty by none other in the world than Fifth Avenue in New York and it must be recognized that she is grandly and richly laid-out. Our coachman can tell us all manner of details about it and points out a castle-shaped house, which cost only two million dollars to build and where a respectable fifty-year-old virgin passes her lonely days. A bit further is the house of a shoemaker who became wealthy and whose income is so large that he has no less than one thousand dollars a day to spend.

We turn right into the wide Bleury and are soon in front of the Church of the Gésu, which is known as one of the nicest buildings in the city and only a few footsteps from there is St. Mary's College, of which the façade is worth seeing. One of the points of interest of the city, especially recommended to us to visit is one of the many cloisters, particularly the Nunnery, which opens its gates for foreigners from 12:00 to 2:00. We thus leave the lively city bustle and arrive in a quiet street in front of the iron fence of a garden, which surrounds a large building. An elderly nun opens the doors for us and lets us inside, into a rather neat and tastefully decorated small church that is still much bigger than many of the Catholic village churches in the Netherlands. In very refined French, she asks us to wait here a few minutes until the afternoon service commences.

The heavy cloister bell has hardly made its twelve muffled bangs heard when, in the back of the little church, a door opens and quietly and solemnly enters a long queue of nuns who walk in pairs up closely to the altar, make the sign of the cross and then, just as correctly as drilled soldiers, take places to the right and left in the pews. The dresses are very simple — a light-grey wide habit covers a bright white garment, of which the sleeves and wimple are visible, and is closed by a belt around the waist. About fifty sisters have already taken their seats when still about thirty younger women in a somewhat different costume (probably novices) enter, and one after another look for their seats.

The Mother Superior, who sits in the back, gives a clearly audible tap on her prie-dieu and immediately starts half-singing, half-reciting, chanting the prayers. The words and sentences are spoken perfectly simultaneously and with completely the same intonation, at once seemingly happy and cheerful, then again almost in a plaintive tone and with profound melancholy. And each time a short break is given, its ending is signalled by a tap from the 'Mother' and the murmuring prayers continue with the same monotony and with the same rhythm.

The solemn service that was held with a peculiar sobriety in the deathly quiet church, where one can hear each breath taken and would be able to hear a pin drop, is soon finished. After well over a quarter of an hour, again at the signal of the headmistress, the women all stand up at the same time and quietly and calmly disappear just

Grey Nunnery Chapel Interior, about 1890

the way they came, the novices in front and then the others joining in military fashion, so that those who entered the temple last, also stayed there the longest.

Now, an older Sister joined us and she requested we follow her. She guided us while conversing pleasantly (and absolutely without overly serious conversation) through a number of rooms where everything excelled in cleanliness and neatness — not a speck of dust was there to detect, no smudges were visible. She told us that all present sisters had forever broken with worldly life. They did not wish so much to isolate themselves to be alone with their God but to be, as much as possible, useful for mankind and also to encourage their own spiritual welfare by helping the poor, the needy and the unfortunate; to lead a God-fearing way of life, and in that way to promote their religion. The worldly purpose then is to educate, in the broadest sense of the word, neglected and needy children, orphans, etc., and to nurse the helpless and sick old men and women.

The good lady was apparently proud of everything she could show us — the large kitchens, where the nuns do their work silently and calmly, the immensely spacious laundry with attached ironing room and drying rooms, the very simple, yet spotless and spacious dining rooms. In short, everything was very neat. Having climbed a few stairs, we arrived at a large room where dozens of children play ball, play marbles, skip rope, etc., and all under the supervision of a few nuns, who join in to their heart's content and are just as cheerful as the youngsters. The children are respectfully candid, and do not run away when one speaks to them. In short, they show the features of being raised in a polite manner.

Now follows the classrooms. The first we enter has about twenty-five girls between the ages of eight to ten years old, who welcome us right away with a nicely performed song, while afterwards little ones recite a verse. It is not without a feeling of pity that I look at one and the other. Why I have sympathy for those poor sheep who are well-dressed and are well-nourished and whose health is painted on their cheeks, I do not know, but with a melancholic feeling, we visit this one and still a few other similar locations. Afterwards, we arrive at the wards where seniors lay waiting for their dying hour. Very, very old men and women, too old and too weak to move, lay there in long rows on snow-white sheets and pillows and with a gauze mask over the face, to keep away the pestering flies.

It was awful to see — no sound was heard, not even from their nursing Sisters, who seemed more to float than to walk. The first impression, then, was not that one had entered a patient chamber but that one had entered a death ward. The emaciated and decrepit patients laid there so frightfully quiet and calm, as if they had already passed away, and the livid colour on faces and hands was so correct and exact, that one of us, a few days later, was still convinced that he truly had walked among some corpses. The devotion went so far that even the mentally ill (provided that they were not violent and rowdy) were tended in this house of God.

We were shown the library, a few rooms where the Sisters could enjoy each other's company after the work is done and before they go to their own cells. One room contained a permanent exhibition of a variety of beautiful needlework, which they had made during their free time. This consisted of ingeniously-made lace as fine as gossamer, masterly made embroideries, lovely artificial flowers and so on. All are on sale for the visitors, not for terribly high prices, but for a price, which is appropriate for the article. After all, a neat bouquet of artificial flowers for the price of ten cents can not be said to be expensive, yet if one wants to pay more, every gift for the benefit of the institution is thankfully accepted, but no pressure is applied.

And so with this, we have seen everything of the cloister that the public is permitted to see. The friendly nun said farewell to us with a markedly affectionate handshake. She wished us a pleasant journey and closed the large gate behind us, giving us the impression that, besides the way religion is praised and served here inside the heavy walls, an awful lot is sacrificed to do good amongst the suffering of the human race and to help it along. With those thoughts in mind, we again take a seat in our landau and forward we go again, through a number of busy streets to the rather large Dominion Square.

This is again one of those pleasant, lovely parks that the English system has introduced into the large cities; a pleasing, leafy footpath, where one can find some quiet diversion without one having to leave one's activities in the bustling street for a long time or to go a great distance. Besides, this square has the great honour to be framed by a row of beautiful buildings, among which the Windsor Hotel certainly holds first place. Although not very high (it is no more than six stories high), it is a colossal corner house for which no costs are spared, so as to transform it as beautifully inside as outside into a palace of riches and luxury that with its stately towers may be called the pride of this park. And nearly opposite this worldly building, at the corner of Cemetery and Dorchester Streets, we find the wonderful St. Peter's Cathedral, of which the beautiful and black-domed tower points so majestically to the heavens.

We now drive out of the city centre in the direction of the high-rigged sailing ships, whose pennants flutter lustily in the air above the houses. Soon, we are at the long harbour that, over a long way, is equipped with sizeable basalt quaywalls, beside which the waterway is so deep that the most heavily-laden ocean steamers can moor at it. Trade seems to be substantial — a multitude of freight and passenger ships, of barques and frigates, are being loaded and unloaded, and give to the surroundings a bustling activity joined with tow-carts and carriages and with steam winches and singing sailors. It is always pleasant to see one or the other close by, especially if one does not run the risk of barging into crates and drums, packages and hawsers.

Montreal Harbour near Custom House, 1865–1875

We pause for a moment at the splendid Custom House, with its high tower from where every movement of the ships can be observed and on which a signal box is also built. Then we start our trip back to our hotel, where we arrive at one o'clock, still just in time for the lunch. And while we ate heartily, Lissone tells us that since the preparation of the itinerary, the travel plans have changed and cannot be exactly executed. If we want to leave tomorrow morning according to plan, then we would inevitably miss a connection with the steamboats crossing Lake Champlain and would have to hang around a whole day in a town not worthy of mention. He asked us to consider whether to travel already this evening and to spend the night in a hotel that is noted as first-rate, and then start tomorrow morning with a series of wonderful steamboat tours.

This proposition caused quite amusing (yet sometimes even rather intense) discussions. One of the ladies has a headache and would rather stay; one of the gentlemen thinks that he has already seen all the nice things of Montreal and that the headache will pass when we are seated again in a train. Someone else thinks that our hotel is not cozy enough to stay there any longer, and yet another, who does not care what we do, sets up the quarreling out of pure pleasure to see them at one another's throats. And when a few had become rather angry and had hurled a few strong reproaches at one another, we proceeded to a vote, whereby it was decided that we should depart at 5 o'clock.

In the remaining time, during which the angry company split into a few parties, a threesome of gentlemen, including me, walk once again into the busy St. James Street to Victoria Square, where we pause for a moment at one of the lovely shaded benches. We choose a nice cool spot, close to a basin, where a number of fountains throw their elegant water streams into the air, and directly opposite to us is the high statue of Albion's powerful Queen, with the simple but telling word 'Victoria', chiselled into the plinth. And all around the lovely foliage, we find again a number of splendid buildings among which the colossal and neatly finished Albert buildings are certainly the nicest, even though the Young Men's Christian Association (bordering the beautiful St. Patricks Hall) in her gothic style and with her slimline spire is also worth mentioning.

After we strolled past the richly displayed shop windows and had purchased some souvenirs here and there, is it time to depart and soon we sit with our luggage in the omnibus that takes us to the large station of the Delaware & Hudson Railroad where we will be inspected by American customs officers. These people are fortunately very accommodating and open up only a few suitcases and when no contraband goods are found, grant permission to load all our belongings. We have soon taken our seats and after waiting a few moments, we hear the signal for departure and we drive off, soon to be outside the city and to stop again at a small train station in the vicinity of the big Railroad Bridge.

It seemed that something was wrong, because there was so much walking up and running down and the train moved so surprisingly slowly, one moment moving a bit, then again stopping. Finally, we were moving forward again and the mystery was soon solved when we noticed beside the rail, a large locomotive lying upside-down. The huge thing seemed to have crashed quite recently, at any rate, smoke and steam still came out of the stacks, if wrecked copper and ironwork can still be called by that name. We are soon on the long Victoria Bridge, of which we did not get to see much, since the whole train moves in a surprisingly long metal tube, where the daylight is permitted only through window openings put here and there.

And after having driven rather quickly for about eight minutes, we come again into the open air, while a muted blow of the steam whistle seemed to tell us that we have left Canada behind us and are moving on United States territory again."

Dominion Square and Y.M.C.A. Building, about 1880

Chapter Eleven

Montreal to Quebec City, 1825

Duke Bernhard of Saxe-Weimar-Eisenach

Duke Bernhard, after seeing Kingston and remarking on its military presence, continued through to Quebec, staying there from September 3 to 9, 1825. He does not demonstrate the same enthusiasm as Schuijlenburg for the cities and facilities. Nevertheless, his appreciation of the natural beauty of the countryside and insight into the culture and military are both very evident.

"At eight o'clock in the evening of September 3, we boarded, together with the gentlemen and ladies Grymes[55] and Clare[56], the steamboat Lady Sherbrooke to travel 180 miles to Quebec. Montreal is lacking in good quays. This we noticed during our departure because were required to wade through deep mud along the shore in the dark — an expedition, which was very unpleasant for the ladies. We had booked so-called staterooms, or special rooms, on this vessel, so that the ladies could withdraw separately and not have to sleep in the common ladies' cabin. It was also pleasant for me to have a room to myself. While in Montreal, I had met with an English artillery captain, King, who I had previously met in Boston and who was also making the trip to Quebec. For the remainder of the trip, except for a few others, our travel company was not very large.

The steamship was 150 feet long with a capacity of eight hundred tons, powered by a sixty-horsepower engine, much too small for such a large and heavy ship. It got under way that evening after nine o'clock. During the night it stopped for an hour at the mouth of the Sorel River, in the St. Lawrence near the town of William Henry — a town that had acquired its name in honour of the Duke of Clarence. They had to take on wood. The engines of the American and Canadian steamships are not fuelled with hard coal like in Europe, but with wood, which takes considerable time to load on board. Toward morning, we stopped along the left bank near the small town of Trois-Rivières, which has twenty-five hundred inhabitants, is eighty miles from Montreal and is situated at the discharge of the St. Maurice into the St. Lawrence. It is built along this river, in which the ebb and flood of the tides are noticeable. Before reaching this place, we had sailed through Lac St. Pierre, which is formed by a widening of the St. Lawrence. Both shores of the river are inhabited and appear well-cultivated and fertile. The river is generally two to three miles wide, but five miles above Trois Rivières, near the village of Richelieu, it narrows, and one finds here the last rapids, Rapids de Richelieu. The shores, which up to here had been fairly flat, especially on the left side, now became higher and rocky. The area is extremely beautiful and picturesque. The majestic river with its friendly shores and the view of the distant Blue Mountains of Quebec had an indescribably captivating impact. The weather was very favourable for us; it was a bright day, with sunshine and not too warm; in this northern climate, the approaching autumn announces itself all too soon with cool nights and mornings.

We arrived in Quebec at ten o'clock that evening. This city has two parts, the upper town, built upon the rock, and the lower town, nestled between the rock and the river. The lights of the lower city provided a magnificent scene, set against the dark rocks on which the fortifications stand. The first view that night reminded me of Namur[57], as seen from the right bank of the Meuse. Many ships lay on the river, most of them employed in the timber trade. As it was already quite late and we had difficulty arranging transportation for the baggage at night, and because it would also prove an inconvenience finding accommodations for the ladies, we decided to remain aboard the steamship, where we felt quite comfortable and enjoyed the greatest cleanliness.

Citadel at Namur, Belgium, 2005

The following morning, after I had dismissed the honour guard that had been lined up near our vessel at the order of the Governor General, we left the ship at seven o'clock and proceeded to our lodgings in the Lemoine Boarding House, located in the upper town. The lower town is very cramped, appears very dirty and old, and does not have paved streets but only poor trottoirs. *A very steep road leads to the upper town. This is built on rocky ground, with its citadel 350 feet above the level of the water. It is separated from the lower town by a crenellated wall, in the form of a hornwork and built upon the rocks. There is a gate in this wall, manned by a guard whose guardroom is directly above the gate, and from where the entrance is covered by means of machicolations. For the comfort of pedestrians, there is a door next to the gate, through which one can get to the upper town by means of a wooden stairway. To the right of the gate is a building resembling a chapel, which serves the lower house of the Canadian Parliament as an assembly hall. We had to proceed for a fair distance along the wall before we arrived at our lodgings; from here, we had an indescribably beautiful view of the bay in front of Quebec and of the right shore of the river, which forms a cape called Pointe Levi.*

Shortly after our arrival, I received visits from Lt. Col. Duchesnay,[58] first adjutant to the Governor General, and from Lt. Col. Durnford,[59] director of the Engineers.

Colonel Elias Durnford, 1861

The former wished to bid me welcome in the name of the Governor, and the latter offered to give me a tour of the fortifications. Lord Dalhousie, Governor General of all British possessions in North America, was on leave in England, but was expected back any day. In his absence, Lieutenant Governor, Sir Francis, the brother of Lord Conynham, was in command of the colony. He is a civilian but, notwithstanding this, renders himself worthy in every respect of this high position. The government must acknowledge that the good spirit reigning in this colony is the result of his humane and friendly conduct toward the local residents. Of Lord Dalhousie, they say he has through his haughtiness and absolute manner distanced himself and the government from the hearts of the people, thus giving the opposition parties in the Canadian Government substantial sway.

Accompanied by both aforementioned staff officers, we began our walking tour, first visiting Government House. This is a large old building which stands empty during the absence of Lord Dalhousie. The rooms were not as large and richly furnished as I would have expected for the residence of a British Governor General. There is a long balcony at the rear of the house, overlooking the gorge, from where one can see a large part of the lower town, the harbours and the surrounding area.

The citadel is a new work, not yet completed. The English speak of the fortification of Quebec with something akin to reverence and consider it equal to the works at Gibraltar. I had thus expected to find something extraordinary; I cannot say, however, that my expectations were rewarded.

Montmorency Falls, 1865

The heights near the city are the widely known Plains of Abraham, or more correctly, Hauteurs d'Abraham, where, on September 12, 1759, the battle between the British General Wolfe and the French General Marquis de Montcalm had taken place. This battle, which had claimed the lives of both generals, had been lost by the French, resulting in the loss of the city — and the entire colony.

Specifically, General Wolfe had occupied the Ile d'Orleans and taken Pointe Levi. The Marquis de Montcalm had stood with his army in a fortified position on the heights near the waterfalls of

Montmorency, from which place he had valiantly repulsed an attack by General Wolfe, with great losses to the British army. Following this, General Wolfe had embarked his army onto ships and at night, under cover of darkness, had sailed under the city and on up the St. Lawrence, landing at the place now called Wolfe's Cove. Here, he had climbed the rocks with much effort and at the break of day had set his army in battle-order on the Hauteurs d'Abraham. In order to come to the defence of the city and to drive the British off the Hauteurs d' Abraham, the Marquis de Montcalm had deemed it necessary to leave his strong unassailable position near Montmorency and to cross the St. Charles River — over a bridge secured by a double bridgehead. He had then positioned his army on the heights with their backs to Quebec, and opened the battle, with the outcome that for him and his government was so tragic.

The British engineers use bricks baked in England for the construction of the casements in the citadel. The cost to the government of transporting a thousand of these bricks comes to two pounds, ten shillings! They say openly that the bricks baked in this country will crack during the local harsh winters; I confess, however, that I have some doubts over these concerns, and I believe their use has some other reason.

The arsenal is a large but not bombproof building, within which they store twenty thousand infantry muskets as well as some very suitable entrenchment guns. We also saw several very handsomely adorned single- and double-barrel guns, intended as gifts to Indian chiefs.

The upper city is also very old and angular with streets that are dirty and, for the most part, not paved. Both cities combined have twenty-five thousand residents. The Catholic cathedral is a very respectable building with three altars and paintings of no great value. Because of the cold climate, it has a wooden floor. Like British churches, the interior is partitioned. It butts against the seminary — a massive old French building with very thick walls and four projecting corners (like a bastion). This seminary includes the residence of the Catholic Bishop of Quebec. We had met Bishop Plessis previously at a social gathering hosted by Sir Francis Burton and had recognized him as a very fine and well-educated man. He is the son of a butcher from Montreal and has elevated himself to this position on his own

*merit. Several years ago, he had undertaken a journey to England,
France and Italy, where he was appointed by the Pope as Archbishop
of Canada; the British government had concerns in approving this
appointment, for as a result of being Archbishop in the Canadian
Parliament, he would have precedence over the Anglican bishop.
We paid this honourable gentleman a visit. He received us in a most
friendly manner, surrounded by several young clergymen. His secretary
showed us around the building and the garden. The seminarians had a
holiday at this time, so there were none in the house. These seminarians
are not all destined for the clergy; many of the distinguished people in
this country send their sons to be educated in this institution, where
they receive very respectable instruction.*

Joseph-Octave Plessis, Bishop of Quebec, 1810

The Catholic clergy are held in high esteem, having earned this through their knowledge and the good deeds they perform. The British government allowed the clergy to retain the emoluments and prerogatives they held before the conquest of the colonies by the English, for which reason they had unconditionally surrendered to the government and now exercise their influence on the people in support of the government. There is a science-room in the seminary, which at present is not yet very comprehensive. It had a small electrical machine, a planetarium, an air pump and a galvanic pillar — with its associated devices. The natural science room is also not very complete: the best exhibit being a collection of East Indian shells. The garden of the seminary is fairly large and serves as a fruit and vegetable garden; it also serves as a walking area, and God knows what else!

On the second and final day of my stay in Quebec I went to a parade, accompanied by Colonels Durnford and Duchesnay. I was pleasantly surprised when I found the entire garrison under arms, each staff-officer wishing to show me his corps. On the right wing stood two companies of artillery, then a company of sappers and miners, and following this, the 68th and, finally, 71st Infantry Regiment. The last, a light regiment consisting of Scottish Highlanders, appeared to be in particularly good order. This regiment does not wear the uniform of the highlanders, only a few pipers that made up the regiment wear it. It had a very good band of buglers, who wore peculiar wool caps — blue in colour, and red-and-white checkered at the bottom. The troops passed by me twice in review, after which I requested they be dismissed.

At six o'clock in the evening of September 6, we proceeded to the steamship Lady Sherbrooke, on which we had arrived the evening two days previous, to return again to Montreal. Sir Francis had put his carriage at our disposal, so that the ladies Grymes and Clare made use of it at the quay. A company of the 68th Regiment with their colours had lined up as an honour guard, which I dismissed immediately. The Fort saluted me with twenty-one guns, which created a very fine echo in the mountains. The ship got under way shortly thereafter. At about this time, night fell but we still had sufficient light to enjoy and bid farewell to the lovely surroundings in which Quebec is situated."

Chapter Twelve
Quebec City and Surroundings, 1859

Willem T. Gevers-Deynoot

"Quebec is a city of about 50,000 souls and, after Montreal, the most populous city in Canada. Because of her strategic location, it is sometimes called the 'Gibraltar of America'. She is split into two parts, a lower and upper town. Quebec is built upon a peninsula or cape, so-called Cape Diamond, which is washed on the right by the St. Lawrence and on the left by the St. Charles River, merging in front of the city, forming a large water mass and shaping an excellent waterfront. The upper town sits on a mountain ridge. A large fortress is built on the highest part that rises more than 300 feet above the river. The lower town winds round her foot, wedged between the rivers and the rock. The city has, therefore, a cluttered appearance, but makes a picturesque sight from a distance. The streets to the upper town are winding and quite steep. A part of the lower town toward the St. Charles is laid out in an orderly manner. There are a number of excellent public buildings, a spacious Roman Catholic cathedral and they were also busy constructing a new Parliament building, since the previous one burned down. The houses are generally low and, although it is very busy, the city was not charming but was sombre and unfamiliar. In the lower town, one still finds complete districts built of wood with streets bordered with planks.

There is a lot of trade in Quebec, particularly in timber that is transported on large rafts from the north and over the St. Lawrence.

Many large merchant vessels and a few steamships that maintain regular service with England (especially those sailing via Glasgow) are berthed in the lower town. Quebec has become the largest gathering place of immigrants. Some of them settle there, and some leave for Montreal and Canada's west. In 1858, 12,810 immigrants arrived in 154 ships, of which 4,412 were male adults. Included were 6,441 English, 1,153 Irish, 1,424 Scots, 922 Germans and 2,656 Norwegians. In 1857, their number had amounted to 32,097 and since 1829, 913,815 immigrants had arrived in Quebec.

Open chairs on high wheels harnessed to a horse with the driver sitting up front in a box, called a calèche, chiefly maintain the connection between the upper and lower town. At home, one calls it a harness race chair with an old-fashioned seat [vooropje]. One sees many carriages driving back-and-forth that one can hire for a small price. As in Montreal, French is very much spoken here. In the streets, one meets Indian women who offer native crafts for sale. Most are made of birch bark or decorated with glass beads. They also sell leather snowshoes called moccasins. Everything was, however, made crudely and more exotic than appealing.

On the highest point behind the city is the fortress. It is very spacious and there, one can enjoy the panorama of the city, the St. Lawrence and the surrounding countryside. This sight is delightful and that alone is worth the trip to Quebec.

Quebec, Typical Caleche

At the fortress was a small British garrison and there were a few signal shot cannons. The British standard flew from the highest point. A bit lower in the city, one finds a small public park where a dilapidated obelisk made from granite stands in honour of Generals Wolfe and Montcalm, former commanders of the English and French. Both perished in 1759 near this city. From this point, one can also enjoy a spectacular panorama.

The area surrounding Quebec is famous for its natural beauty. Moreover, the shores of the St. Lawrence and the Saguenay River below the city are also supposed to have striking natural scenery. We visited the well known, and for that matter no less spectacular, Montmorency Falls located eight miles from Quebec. An enchanting road at some distance from the St. Lawrence goes down there. We passed a large mental hospital, where we saw a group of the unfortunates working the land. A little further down the road stands a small marble column, decorated with a large cross. I read the inscription. It is a memorial erected in appreciation for the good work of a temperance society, which was established a few years ago by a French priest. On the other side was a strange inscription: "O Jesus! À qui on ne donna que du vinaigre et de l'hysope!" One drives through a large village called Beauport (still completely inhabited by French people) and finally arrives at a country house, where for a fee of one shilling, entrance is given to the famous waterfall.

The Montmorency is a small river, sixty feet wide, that plunges 250 feet straight down between the rocks to flow a little further on into the St. Lawrence. The falls are wild and create a surprising amount of turbulence, but one could miss much of the scene unless one goes by a very long difficult detour to get to the foot of the falls, something that is required at all waterfalls. Above the fall, the flow of Montmorency is still blocked by naturally carved rock masses. A few years ago, a suspension bridge was built over the fall; now, one can only see the pillars. Shortly after the opening, the bridge collapsed while a man with his horse and wagon and two pedestrians were on it. Everything was crushed by the fall, and it was decided not to repair the bridge. We returned along the same path to Quebec, looking beautiful with her shining tin roofs lit by the sun.

That same day we visited the famous Plains of Abraham, on the other side of Quebec. It was here, west of the fortress alongside the St. Lawrence that, on September 13, 1759, the big battle against the French took place, which decided the destiny of Canada. No Englishman will omit going here and visiting the small column erected at the spot where General Wolfe was shot down. The well from which he drank for the last time also is shown. It is irrefutable that the military manoeuvre of this English general who, while sailing past Quebec put his troops ashore here, is amongst the most daring of military tactics. He did manage to completely defeat the surprised French, but according to my judgment, this fact is idealized too much. It is in Canada with Wolfe, like it is in England with Nelson.

Our plan was to travel from Quebec to Niagara. We were advised to sail to it on the St. Lawrence River and since it was portrayed as being attractive, we decided to proceed that way. For the various steamboats necessary for the trip, one could purchase tickets in Quebec, which also took care of the transport of the baggage. The journey would most likely take three days and three nights, which cost no more than twelve dollars per head, including meals. Thus, we said farewell to Quebec to travel again west bound into Canada."

To the Laurentians and Back to Quebec City, 1877

Gerrit Verschuur

As did most of the travellers, the brothers Gerrit and Wouter Verschuur spent some time in Quebec City, of which they were greatly enamoured. Both likely considered themselves Francophiles. They had left Holland behind and settled respectively in France and Switzerland.[60] Belonging to the upper middle-class, they were experienced travellers. Moreover, after the death of their father,

Gerrit Verschuur

it became Gerrit's way of life. He published a number of books in French documenting his journeys to far away and often exotic lands across the globe. In addition to his books, the World Museum in Rotterdam maintains his extensive collection of ethnographic artifacts. His photographs from his tour through Canada are amongst them.[61]

The brothers shared much of this journey with fellow world-traveller, Giovanni Tomasoni, a lawyer from Padua, Italy[62]. In addition to their visit to Quebec City, they were also compelled to make a side-trip along Saguenay River to the rugged and majestic Laurentian Mountains.

"While I was being told that the location of this city [Quebec City] was so picturesque that she brought to mind the Gulf of Naples, and that her solid position on the rocks was comparable to Gibraltar, I considered this depiction as being exaggerated. However, when I went up on deck at 6 o'clock in the morning, I found that the truth had been spoken. Quebec is majestic and scenic located upon a hill in a spacious and wide bay, where everything in the distance is green. Quebec is wonderfully situated!

We saw the citadel high up the hill, representing the historical part of the city. Which role has Quebec really played in history? That of a city which over and over again was taken and retaken, and has been the centre of the battles that decided the destiny of Canada. The citadel was built in 1609. Champlain made it the centre of his operations. Under the powerful influence of this viceroy, the colony developed rapidly and ten years after the establishment of the fortress, Quebec counted already a few thousand residents. But, soon being involved in war with England, the city surrendered in 1629. In 1632, it returned to the possession of France under the peace treaty, which provided for Charles I of England to give Canada back to Louis XIII.

Since that time and until 1689, when a new war with England broke out, the colony developed quickly. Trois-Rivières, Ottawa and

Frontenac [Kingston] were founded; and Canada increased its trade more and more. Only the war with the Indians had disturbed the peace of the country, but these hordes only appeared between long intervals. Many tribes had already signed alliances with the French. After hostilities between the two countries had resurfaced, in 1690, Quebec once again had to withstand an attack from the English. Fire from the citadel ravaged the English fleet in such a way that they retreated in a hurried fashion.

Since then, the city had not played a war-waging role in the French-English battles until 1759, when Montcalm, after having maintained the battle for a long time against a superior enemy, was forced to withdraw to Quebec. Since the citadel fully protected his encampment, he reckoned his army to be invincible and his position impregnable. Just like many generals, he was to become the victim of treason. After a first unsuccessful attempt, the English General, Wolfe, had to change his strategy. Two deserters of the French army handed him the countersign, and so General Wolfe was able to cross his army over the St. Lawrence River during the night and occupy the heights, known by the name 'the Plains of Abraham'.

When the news about it became known in the French camp, Montcalm ordered his army to march forward and to attack the English. The English were protected by walls which they had put up in the night, and opened a murderous fire at a distance of 50 yards that created chaos and terror among the ranks of the French. Montcalm, however, severely injured, instilled courage into his soldiers and tried to reorganize them. Wounded again, this time mortally, he fell from his horse and his body was taken to the city. On the enemy side, General Wolfe also died, but with the self-satisfaction that the battle had taken a turn to his advantage.

This rich country had been for one-and-a-half centuries in French possession and, as a result of that battle, it returned to English hands. One main cause was certainly the lack of the necessary troops, along with the indifference of Louis XV, who cared less about the destiny of his soldiers than about the pleasures his ParcauxCerfs would give him.

Upon our return, we would stop in Quebec and transfer directly to another steamboat, the Saguenay, which promptly departed to Northern Canada, first by the St. Lawrence River and later by the

Saguenay River. The St. Lawrence River, in particular, passes Quebec with such a wide berth that one forgets they are sailing on a river and one imagines oneself on a vast lake. In the distance, the lushly foliated mountains are barely visible, and a school of dolphins accompanies us for some distance. It is not uncommon that one sees whales in the St. Lawrence. While we were all sitting on deck in a temperate summer heat, Mister Tomasoni becomes ecstatic about the resemblance of the countryside, which we see around us, with that of Lake Maggiore and the surrounding areas of Nice and Genoa. A mail boat catches up with us. It had left an hour after us, destined for Liverpool and, of course, sailing faster than we do will soon pass us. Just as on the open sea, two large sail ships in full sail cross us. We call at a few small towns and steam on the Saguenay River, which is much smaller, surrounded on both sides by mountains and steep rocks, which here and there by the shadow they cast give the water a colour as black as ink. It is melancholic and exotic, but a wonderful spectacle and majestic nature at nightfall, because it is past seven o'clock, when we left the St. Lawrence. We moored for a short time at Tadoussac[63], les Eboulements, and Rivière-du-Loup, at which places we shall stay on our trip back and where we will have the opportunity to look at the salmon breeding and the small lakes with trout. At present, our houseboat moves swiftly forward and ends her journey in St. Alphonse, where we arrive at sunrise in the early morning.

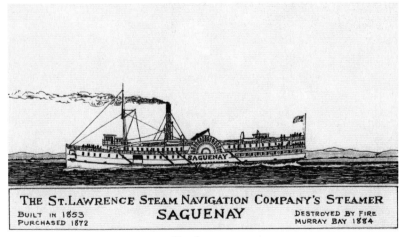

THE ST. LAWRENCE STEAM NAVIGATION COMPANY'S STEAMER
BUILT IN 1853   SAGUENAY   DESTROYED BY FIRE
PURCHASED 1872   MURRAY BAY 1884

The *Saguenay*

The vessel shall stay there until eight o'clock. At five o'clock we were already ashore and in a Canadian village where fishing is the only livelihood. A few wooden houses and a church mainly built from clay, as if all were erected between the rocks, make up the complete village, which looks shabby but which also has such a strange cachet that it touches all of us. We imagine ourselves in the high north, these thoughts greatly stimulated by the cold that prevails in this area. The bay where St. Alphonse is located is named Ha! Ha! Bay, as the Indians called it when they discovered the inlet in the river. In the last years, during the two months when it gets hot in the summer, it is the destination of an excursion such as we are making now.

In all of Canada, the winter on average is cold and sometimes exceptionally severe. The snow often lays six feet high and it is not rare that one can still skate in the month of May. But when the cold makes way, one does not have a lengthy transition from winter to summer and in an incredibly short time everything is green.

During the winter season, Canada is the land of festivities and amusements, where ice sports play an important part. As soon as the cold sets in, water is carried some distance from the city and covered with a wooden structure. The water freezes and gets the shiniest and smoothest surface that one can imagine. Near the time of carnival, these structures are decorated with flags and ribbons, chandeliers are hung up and one dance follows the other.

The upper classes of society go there and one sees the most expensive and most diverse costumes. The tones of the music make themselves heard and soon, one can witness the spectacle of a quadrille performed on skates.

How gladly I would have witnessed such a feast but there was too much of a difference between the temperature that we experienced and the months of the year when these feasts are held.

It must be just as strange as it is an enchanting scene, according to what has been told to me about it, when the beautiful dresses, by the thousands of lights of the chandeliers, are reflected in the shining ice. These skating balls often go on late into the night. There is a friendly atmosphere that never deteriorates into lawlessness.

I let myself be carried away by my sensations. My journey through Canada and the impressions which I treasured would give me enough material for a complete book. Yet our vessel departs from St. Alphonse and here and there we see now in the daylight the picturesque wild nature that we passed at night going in the opposite direction. One informs us that many of the mountains and rocks are of volcanic origin and earthquakes often occur.

The Captain whistles the steam pipe repeatedly, allowing us to hear the strong echo, which reverberates from the rock faces. He also gives us enough time to visit at the fishing and countryside places mentioned before. They are curious villages, and Rivière-du-Loup (where we stay for three hours) especially is very unusual, because we have the opportunity to visit a Canadian Indian village at a short distance from here. What sorts with their black hair? They speak a kind of Frenchslang, of which we only understand half; they are good-natured and allow us to enter their dwellings and to observe the exotic interior of these huts.

The next morning at six o'clock we are again moored at Quebec."

Return to Quebec City, 1811

Klaas Jacobs Kuipers

Long before the Brothers Verschuur (and indeed most of the gentlemen in this book) travelled in comfortable style as well-heeled pleasure-seekers, their fellow countryman, Klaas J. Kuipers, had already sailed down the St Lawrence to Quebec City. In 1811, he served as an experienced sailor on an English ship out of London. His short account is surprisingly rich with details of the life and industry of the town as it was then.

"I left the city of London [England] again [in 1811] on the three-master Prospect, commanded by Captain William Weak and destined for Quebec, the capital of Canada. At the beginning of

May, we reached the point where the Gulf of St. Lawrence flows out of the northeastern part of North America near the island of Newfoundland. One night we encountered three patches of ice. The watchman in the front of the ship shouted,

"Icebergs"! We manoeuvred through pieces of crumbling icebergs, also noticing the cold temperature. At dawn, we sailed into the Gulf of St. Lawrence, which has been estimated to be seventy-five German miles[64] long. On the right-hand or starboard side, located high above sea level, one first passes uninhabited Anticosti Island, being largely covered with snow. Further on, one sails to Silver Island where one receives a pilot to continue on up the river to Montreal. One can hear the noise of a waterfall a long time ahead and then one is confronted with it, an extremely nice scene to see, waterfalls that plunge eighty feet down on the rocks which makes a surprising noise between the high hills. Then, one sees in the distance the city of Quebec, located on a high hill.

The city of Quebec is the capital of all of English Canada. The other part of this land is called 'the free Canada', which is inhabited by first Indian tribes. We moved past the city, up the river into Wolfe's Cove, where we anchored. The pilot was taken in a sloop to the city, as was the captain, taking his required paperwork with him in order to clear customs.[65] There, in order to make the ship ready for loading, the ballast was put with ropes into barges. However, we had to wait eight days before we could start loading. The reason for this was that the masts we were to load came from a great distance in rafts along the river from Montreal, taking about three hundred hours from a certain lake located in the interior of Canada. When a large raft arrives, it is moored up on the riverbank, and then each mast is rolled on the flat shoreline to be cut into a ready-made mast. The labourers had put up tents against the hillside where they spent the night. We had made things ready on board, one spindle to lift into the hold, the other to load on the front deck, for which we had hired Canadian farmers. We had to use a lot of force to heave masts of ninety-six feet into the ship. This is understandable as the bottom girth was thirty-six inches, in the middle it was twenty-two inches and at the top it was eighteen inches. We stayed here for three months before we finished loading the cargo of masts into the vessel.

View of Quebec from timber base at Montmorency about 1810

Having the opportunity, I visited the city including its higher parts to view her interesting sights. If one approaches the city from the back of Wolfe's Cove, one sees green pastures. I noticed some fairly heavy oxen grazing in the pasture but they cannot, by far, match the Dutch breed in beauty and weight. Here and there, one sees large stones on the ground, amongst them one marking where General Wolfe had died during the attack on the city. Still, with the siege, the British nonetheless conquered the city. The victory, I was told, took place in the year 1759. If one walks further inside the gate, one notices a straight street. The buildings in the lower city are not big.

On the left hand at a corner house of a side street, on top of a wall, one sees the sculpture of the fallen General Wolfe, carved in stone, life-size, in memory of the victory. The country Canada earlier belonged to the French crown, however the British have governed it for fifty-five years.[66]

In the suburbs, I saw the foundation stone being laid of a Roman Catholic Church that was being built on the slope of a hill.[67] The ladies and gentlemen deposited lots of gold money and also heavy silver pieces at the foot of the stone which was coloured blue and hollowed out. After we had gazed for a short while at the money, we left the custodians with the money because to stay here any longer would not have made us rich, anyway. But it did arouse our desire, which would not be fulfilled. Walking on, we arrived at the top of the hill where the main church was located and where we stumbled upon more tall buildings.

The view was nice from here, especially because of the high placement of the city on a hill. There were also powerful batteries with heavy guns that could reach the enemy on the opposite riverside from over the city. We walked down the hill to the city's waterfront. One has to descend almost seventy stairs, and then one also finds a few large buildings. However, before one has reached the quay, one still has to climb down almost fifty stairs more. Then one arrives in a long street, behind which the quay is located and used by the ships that are loaded with mixed cargo. Here, we even met countrymen who had arrived on English merchant ships. We slowly strolled along the riverside to board our ship, but we had to be picked up with a sloop in order to get on board. We had amused ourselves very well that day, which resulted in a good night's sleep. That day we were not loafing — being driven by curiosity, we had kept walking.

The next morning, the second [navigation] officer again awakened us, and everybody was allocated his chores because there are always work routines to be carried out on a ship.

We had the time to provide what was needed for the ship's rigging. My activities consisted of painting with a brush and swabbing the decks.

The second officer, wanting to leave the sea, went ashore on the sloop and was press-ganged by the British Navy and forced to board a war-frigate. After that, the captain asked me to take up his post. It was well-known to our Captain that I had sailed before in the capacity of first [navigation] officer on Dutch and Prussian vessels. The biggest problem for me was that I did not have command of the English language. It was also my first trip, but I worked diligently to learn as much English as possible.

After a month had gone by, my fellow countryman Jan Brand (born on the island of Texel) and I had the opportunity to go ashore again to visit Canadian farmers. We walked along the hills through the valleys and glens. Here, one finds some farmer households which are mixed marriages; for example, an Englishman married to a Canadian woman whose children can speak both English and French. There are still a few Indians there who navigate their canoes (in other words small boats) along the river. It's wonderful to see how skilfully they can manoeuvre these canoes. When arriving on shore, they raise them onto their shoulders and put them in a friend's shed to prevent them from getting damaged. The canoes are mostly fabricated from sealskin and whalebones.

The fertility of the land did not disappoint me and at that point it seemed to me not very rocky in the valleys. The heads of the grain were very full. One finds only small farms here. Nothing is imported for the daily necessities of the inhabitants, also little of the agricultural production is transported elsewhere, which means that the inhabitants take care of their own needs, mainly with the products from their land. Thus we both had made a pleasurable trip, and I should not forget to mention that we also had treated ourselves with cream from a Canadian farmer's wife. She charged us quite a lot for it. In Dutch money, it amounted to one guilder per person, but we paid it anyway. Towards evening, we finally went on board the ship. The sloop was lying on the riverbank and we sailed with the other crew members to our ship. Soon afterwards, we received our cargo, the sails were hoisted and everything was made ready for our departure. We left Quebec City for England on the Prospect on August 28, 1811."

Chapter Thirteen

Quebec City to Montreal, 1825

Duke Bernhard of Saxe-Weimar-Eisenach

Formality and fanfare often greeted Duke Bernhard during his journey through Canada. This high-ranking Dutch army officer writes in detail about these occasions, apparently taking it all in stride. More significantly, he provides a precise personal record and his point of view about the local inhabitants and their social circumstances, contrasting the lifestyles of those of privilege with settlers and other emigrants.

"At six o'clock in the evening of September 6, we proceeded to the steamship Lady Sherbrooke, on which we had arrived the evening two days previous, to return again to Montreal. Sir Francis Burton[68] *had put his carriage at our disposal, so that the ladies Grymes and Clare made use of it. At the quay, a company of the 68*th *Regiment, with their colours, had lined up as an honour guard, which I dismissed immediately; the fort saluted me with twenty-one guns, which created a very fine echo in the mountains. The ship got underway shortly thereafter. At about this time, night fell but we still had sufficient light to enjoy and bid farewell to the lovely surroundings in which Quebec is situated.*

The journey upstream naturally went slower, as we were proceeding against the flow of the river. Fortunately, a high tide that night helped us over the Rapids de Richelieu. We stopped at

Trois-Rivières in the morning to take on wood. After that, our progress was slow. I used this time of leisure for writing but was often interrupted. Specifically, on this vessel they had four meals daily and with each meal, they drove me from my place of writing. In the morning at seven o'clock, they sound the bell for rising and dressing; at eight, they have breakfast — tea and coffee, sausage and ham, beefsteak and eggs; at twelve, there is luncheon; at four o'clock, dinner; at eight o'clock they drink tea; and for every meal the table is set one hour early. The weather was cloudy the entire day and toward evening it rained; it rained continuously the entire night.

In the afternoon, we landed near Sorel, or William Henry, to let off some passengers and take on wood. This place lies at the confluence of the Sorel, or Richelieu — the only outlet for Lake Champlain — and the St. Lawrence, on the right bank of both streams. The French had built a fort here, still standing, if one can refer to such poor palisades surrounding a barracks and a government magazine by calling it a 'fort'. The place had been founded in the year 1785 by American so-called Loyalists and retired soldiers. It has two churches and six hundred inhabitants who live in about one hundred houses, mostly of wood construction, which stand separately along streets that cross at right angles and form large squares. It had been built on sandy soil and has a poor appearance. On the whole, the towns in Canada, in comparison to those in the United States, have a poor aspect and will never achieve the same standing, since the settlers in Canada are primarily poor Scots and Irishmen, who came here at the cost of the government, received land and were then placed under the burden of the feudal system, which suppressed all aspirations. Emigrants, on the other hand, who wish to make a start on something and who have an enterprising spirit, settle in the United States, where they are not suppressed, but rather, where everything contributes much more to their advancement.

A detachment of the 70th Regiment is garrisoned in Fort Sorel, under the command of a sergeant. An artillery detachment, moving their artillery requisitions by sloop to Montreal, tied their sloop to our steamship and came onboard. Most of the gunners were drunk. Toward evening, to our significant alarm, we discovered that there were three crates of gunpowder in the boat. The danger was amplified because of the sparks constantly flying from the stack of our steam engine and being blown by the wind down onto the sloop. I was one of the first to acquire this information and raised the alarm immediately. The entire travel company agreed and we induced the Captain to place the arsenal commander and three of his least drunk gunners into the sloop and, in the midst of a rainy and stormy night, have them distance it from our ship. The night, by the way, was so dark that we were forced to drop anchor and lay over for the duration.

The weather the following morning was still cloudy, with rain. The current was extremely strong and the wind also blew directly against us. The engine was too weak to drive us forward, and thus we had Montreal in sight for three hours without being able to attain the city; indeed, the current between Montreal and the island of St. Helen was so strong as to actually drive us backward, despite our engine. Six oxen and two horses were finally set to the task and, with this, an additional ten people also pulled. The Lady Sherbrooke, however, is one of the oldest steamships on the St. Lawrence, and even the Captain confessed she was so decayed as to be no longer worth repair and that she would soon be demolished. At about four o'clock that afternoon, after we had taken forty-six hours for a journey that downstream had taken twenty-six, we landed in Montreal.[69] *The battery on the island of St. Helen saluted us with twenty-one guns. We took up residence once again in our former quarters at the Masonic Hall Hotel.*

Charlotte de Lotbinière,
wife of William Bingham

The first news we received was that yesterday, before noon, fifty houses had burned in the suburbs of the town, and that this accident had befallen the poorest citizens of the city whose houses are seldom insured.

A Mr. Bingham[70] *from Philadelphia, who married a rich heiress here and who had become a Catholic in order to obtain her possessions, today gave a ball in honour of the first birthday of his daughter, and was kind enough to invite our company.*

We accepted the invitation, and at nine o'clock went to the ball. The man is twenty-four and his wife is nineteen years of age. He has many friends, for he possesses a very fine cellar and had the talent to spend his money liberally among the people. We found the entire fashionable society of Montreal gathered in his rich and tastefully furnished drawing room. They danced mostly the French quadrille, and also the so-called Spanish dance. They had adapted dull Scottish melodies to the quadrille, to honour the officers of the 70th Regiment, who are the jeunes gens par excellence of the local city; they played German music to the Spanish dances. The local ladies, our young and pretty hostess included, spoke the local poor French. My attention was particularly drawn to a Miss [Frances] Ermatinger[71], the daughter of a Swiss man and an Indian woman, because of her unusual yet truly pretty Indian face. She was tastefully dressed and danced particularly well. On the whole, the ball was quite animated. At Mr. Bingham's house (whose sister [Anne Louise] was the wife of the banker Alexander Baring in London, England, but had already left her husband), great luxury was prevalent, particularly in silver and crystal items."

Montreal, 1845

Johan C. Gevers

In 1845, before becoming Minister Resident in Stuttgart, Germany, Johan C. Gevers, the Dutch *chargé d'affaires* to the USA, conducted a tour through Canada. He made a few general observations about the country and wrote very little about the cities. We can only assume that Montreal alone was of sufficient interest to him to warrant a few paragraphs. His brief to the Minister of Foreign Affairs about the Montreal portion of his Canadian excursion provides an official but nevertheless valuable comment on Montreal before Confederation.

"The commercial trade of the cities of Montreal and Quebec along the St. Lawrence is substantial. The businesses are partially held in the hands of Americans who can settle here.

Montreal has close to 50,000 residents. The city is quite nice, although it makes a sombre impression. The seat of the government generates activities. There is also the financial heart of the famous Hudson's Bay Company, which was established two centuries ago based on a charter issued by Charles II (in 1672). This charter grants

Johan C. Gevers

the exclusive right to set up a factory for hunting and trade in fur around Hudson's Bay and the adjacent rivers. For a long time, the Company remained in possession of that privilege without anybody giving a thought to challenge her about it, but in 1787 a competing company was established in Canada. The two companies soon engaged in public hostility and they committed reciprocal looting, obligating the English Parliament to intervene in 1821. A new exclusive claim that exists up to date was granted to the Hudson's Bay Company. The territory she operates within stretches out over all British possessions in the northern part of America, from Labrador straight to the Pacific Ocean. In addition, the Company has leased a strip of land for 20 years from the Russian government that borders on Sitka and cuts off the linkage of the English territories with the sea. Two thousand otter hides are given annually for the hunting rights to the St. Petersburg fur trade. There exists a contract whereby Russia commits itself to regularly deliver a certain number of hides to the government of China, some of which are being sold for the price of 200 to 400 dollars. The otters of good quality are only in the Russian possessions.

The head office of the Hudson's Bay Company is in London. There, all transactions are executed with respect to purchasing and shipping of goods that accommodates the fur exchange.

The yearly value of those that are directly imported from the Bay has decreased and is currently estimated at no more than one million dollars. The net profits of the Company are nevertheless substantial. The shares (of which the initial price was £100) are listed at more than a 100% premium; each year a 10% dividend is paid, while a surplus exists that serves as a reserve fund.

The Canadian law (in reality English law) governs the territory and the people, independent from the Hudson's Bay Company. Misdemeanours are judged and punished by assigned servants. Criminals are brought before Canadian courts.

Six thousand hunters or drifters are in the service of the Hudson's Bay Company; almost all are English or Scottish Canadians. Everywhere where they have stayed, one notices through the medley of races in various areas that Indian blood has deteriorated to the point of vanishing. A tribe from the northwest, the Bois-Brûlés [Sichangu], being only in name 'Indian', is composed of almost 40,000 people who descended from employees of the Company. Five hundred of them from ages 18 to 35 years are trained for the regular cavalry. They can read and write and they are educated in such a way, so that, if necessary, they can operate by recruiting and training Indian troops. In case of difficulties at the border with Oregon, such an army would be devastating for the United States.

Every year, employees organize and protect the work activities of the drifters, leaving from Montreal in Indian canoes with 12 rowers. They go along Lakes Ontario, Erie and Huron, past the waterfalls of St. Marie at Lake Superior and make their way over the Winnipeg and Severn Rivers, to Hudson Bay.

Attacks are no longer to be feared from the Indians. The scattered fortresses are adequate for the protection of the Hudson's Bay Company employees. Real skirmishes are exceptional and the greater number of Indians who trade at these forts (with the Hudson's Bay Company) are docile and are involved with the hunt.

Quebec is picturesque and situated on a jutting rock at the banks of the St. Lawrence. There is a lively trade in lumber for construction; more than 2,000 English ships are engaged with the lumber shipping.

The position of Quebec is very solid and the fortifications are kept in good condition. On purpose, I made a point of travelling through the Plains of Abraham, where in 1795 Wolfe became victorious in a bloody battle that took place near the wall of the fortress, and which secured the possession of the Canadas for England.

Lord Charles T. Metcalfe, 1844

In total, there are now 9,000 British troops in the colony, under the command of Lord Cathcart. The troops are garrisoned in Quebec, Montreal, Kingston and Toronto and in various small towns in the two Canadas.

While in Montreal, the anniversary of the Battle of Waterloo was being celebrated with a parade, at which I was present. Last evening, I had a grand ceremonial dinner with Lord Metcalfe."

Montreal, 1866

Claude A. Crommelin

Claude August Crommelin's tour in the USA was presumably for business reasons, at least partly to check on companies into which Dutch money had been invested. He took only a week of his American tour to travel through Canada. On Saturday, July 28, 1866, he changed ships at Ogdensburg in New York state while on his way from Port Charlotte, now the Port of Rochester, to Montreal.

Claude A. Crommelin

"At Ogdensburg, we switched our boat and now steam fast down the St. Lawrence River and through several rapids. The most prominent rapids are Long Sault, Cedar and Lachine. Have most of the rocks been cleared or is it only me that thinks that the so highly commended rapids do not impress me as much as I had anticipated of them? At any rate, I did not, in fact, feel a sense of danger. However, it is undeniable that there is something turbulent and wild in it that makes an impression. I was especially moved by the unusual way the very calm river suddenly, without any apparent reason, changes into a wild sea. The reason for this must be the rocks in the channel — it is surely not only the steep drops that occur only at a few places. The rocks also cause all large waves in the rapids to flow upstream. The shock must be great and one should not forget that for those who sail downstream, especially on a steamer, the stream always seems to flow slowly. The banks of the St. Lawrence River are more developed than I expected and were, in that aspect, disappointing.

Victoria Bridge, 1870

Entering Montreal is a glorious event, yet the sight of the huge tubular bridge especially touched me. One and one-quarter English miles long, it rests on 24 stream pillars and two land abutments, for a total cost of $7,000,000. I stayed in the St. Lawrence Hall."[72]

Sunday, July 29, 1866

"Wrote letters. Toured "round the mountain". The location of Montreal is lovely. It is at the foot of Mount Royal, half-way on a mountain and spread out along the broad river. Most of the houses look tidy and neat, however, not high. In almost all streets, both sides are planted with trees which gives it a homey but, at times, a somewhat dull appearance. The quay along the river is beautiful; however, the view of the river is not always clear because of the many piers, ships and steamboats situated in front of it. Even so, because the quay is quite high, the view is not obstructed as much as it is at Rotterdam."

Monday, July 30 to Wednesday, August 1, 1866

"Grey Nunnery and other sights, they did not mean much to me. In the evening, we sailed on a steamboat to Quebec, where we arrived at 7 o'clock in the morning."

Montreal, 1877

Gerrit Verschuur

While staying in Montreal, G. Verschuur, once again revelled in the "Frenchness" of this city in 1877. The entries about Canada in his book end with this sentiment: "And now, farewell Canada! We remember with pleasure your fecund soil, your magnificent St. Lawrence, your lovely scenery, your warm-hearted inhabitants! Alexander Dumas has not unjustly called them, '*le people le plus hospitalier du monde*'."

"The location of Montreal is rather picturesque. It pleases us again to see a city that looks likes a European one, and thus provides a desired change from all those endless long, identical and straight streets of American cities. "La voiture, Monsieur! Quel hotel, Monsieur?" It is as if we set ashore at Le Havre or Bordeaux, and in Hôtel Richelieu[73], upon our arrival, we see happy, friendly people around us and we find a good French table with good wines. I mentioned before, that we had notified a few friends about our arrival in Montreal. They were two law scholars, the gentlemen M. and L., with whom we became

Richelieu Hotel, Montreal

acquainted in Italy (along with the family S.) and who we, after having travelled together for fourteen days, had left and, just as we did with the family S. from Cleveland, had given the assurance to visit them soon in their own country. Circumstances can often take a strange turn. The day after we had parted from both gentlemen in Naples, they joined Giovanni Tomasoni, a travelling companion from Padua, Italy and shared his companionship for three weeks. He also had the intention to visit America next year and promised at that occasion in Montreal to renew the acquaintance.

Just as it had been in our case, their intended plan became a reality. A few days after the announcement that we were on our way, a letter arrived from the friend in Padua and, the day before we arrived by steamboat in Montreal, he had arrived there by railway.

The character of the 'French-Canadians' was already a sufficient guarantee for the warm welcome that awaited us.

The coincidence made a feast of our stay as well as that of the easy-going corpulent Padua gent, with whom we were soon on equal terms

Statue of Giovanni Tomasoni, Padua, Italy

as if we had already known him for years. All of our time was taken up. Everything was already arranged before our arrival. We did not have anything to say. The carriages were hired and the whole program was made for the three days, which we had earmarked for Montreal. Our new friend Tomasoni, active earlier in Padua as lawyer and now living there off his investments, at the age of 53 made once again a trip around the world. He was only on American territory a few weeks and would travel from San Francisco to Japan. For that tour, he had put aside two years so he would be able to take it at his own speed.

I have seldom encountered anyone of his age with such a joie de vivre, such inexhaustible strength and still so young in spirit as that man, who gave from morning to evening the impression of someone who is only after having a good time. Signor Tomasoni[74] is over the moon that we know Padua so well and can converse with him about the 'Sala Dei Pedrocchi' and the Saint Antonio. We definitely have to visit him, when he returns from his trip.

The hotel in Montreal could present only a small bill to us because, except for the afternoon meal at our arrival, our hosts only allowed us to sleep there. Their carriage drives us home, or it is ready to pick us up. The corpulent Mr. Tomasoni declares continuously with a stream of words that he has never encountered so much politeness and we fully agree with that sentiment.

Montreal is a city with a friendly façade, clean streets (which are better paved than the American ones), proper stores, a spacious park (Victoria Park), and giving an overall impression of a city in France. From a long road, located high outside the city, one has the most beautiful view of the surroundings.

She is situated in the middle with her shining roofs and spires (the reason why the author Francois Chateaubriand gave her this epithet, "la ville aux toits d'argent") and the wide St. Lawrence fades away right and left on the horizon.

A doctor, the brother-in-law of Mr. L., whom we met the first evening at dinner, shows us the prison and the mental hospital, that look similar to the many buildings of that kind which I have seen in other countries. It is unnecessary to say how distressing it is to have to leave our hospitable friends. Who knows if we will see them ever again?"

Montreal, 1892

Karel D. W. Boissevain

Karel D.W. Boissevain, 1898

Karel D. W. Boissevain produced a detailed perspective of Montreal in a piece he wrote for a Dutch newspaper. Born into a wealthy family of Dutch financiers, he was no stranger to the finer things in life. After first having spent some time working in Crowsnest Pass, Alberta, he and his family stayed for about eight years in Montreal. He was closely related to the formidable banker Adolphe A. H. Boissevain, who in 1883 played a pivotal role in assisting the CPR with its financing and was consequently well-connected to the Montreal elite. During his time in Canada, Karel Boissevain held a position as the secretary of Alaska Feather & Down Company for a number of years. Coming from a position of privilege, he was also given the opportunity to represent his country for a short time as its Consul-General. His point of view as someone who had become established in Canada comes through in his newspaper articles, as he discussed various facets of life in Montreal as the 19th century came to a close.

"Returning from my winter campaign in the Rocky Mountains, my advance eastwards brought me again gradually approaching the winter. I had left it behind in the Crows Nest Pass and found it again in Manitoba and Quebec. Montreal was still steeply wrapped in its wooly winter cloth and it fitted the city well.

The police decree was still in force that "all transport by axle will be stopped until further notice" and that "all horses, oxen, hinnies or dogs used as beasts of burden or harnessed on vehicles should be provided with bells, which while moving tingle happily and are well audible". And so they did. For a foreigner, it was a continuous expression of cheerfulness, well in harmony with the flushed winter complexion on the faces of the passers-by and with the lively fast trot of the horses. The light, open sledge gives almost no resistance on the hard, cracked dry snow. The light load of the harness is taken off of the horses and when they trot, it is a feast for the eyes and enjoyment for the ear.

Buffalo robes and bear skins cover the seats and the back pillows of the sledges with their furry warmth, hanging over the back and on the sides, and the flaps wave in the wind; the tall bearskin hats of the coachman and their lovely furs of fox or wolf pelts fit so warmly and lovely, and the fur astrakhan that is the general dress on the street, gives an impression of prosperity and luxury. Montreal in the winter is an attractive city!

The residents of the Utrechtschestraat and the Leidschestraat [in Amsterdam], who had to beg for so long for asphalt in front of their doors, would have called Montreal at that time "the paradise of the shopkeepers". No wheel to see in the whole city, even the omnibuses move on sledges, the high beautiful sun and the lovely dry air gets everyone onto the street and the silver sound of the bells seems to work infectiously at the money and the purse. It dances in the pockets! However, it is a pity that this trick does not happen.

If the shopkeepers were to depend on what "dances in the pockets", they would not become wealthy. The largest coin in circulation is a 50-cent piece, and upwards, everything is paper: paper dollars, paper two-dollars, five-dollars, etc. I miss our two-and-a-half-guilders and especially our beautiful gold ten-guilders coin.

Montreal, April 26, 1892

We enjoy the lovely sunny weather here! It must appear to you that I am a youthful son of the soil for the first time at a mayor's reception in the capital, and when introduced to one and the other, as a preamble to dutiful conversation, I make a remark about the weather and again assure every foreigner that it today, or yesterday, or last week, has thawed or blown or rained. Yes, I even fear that it snows here in the winter and thaws in the spring.

Yet for a foreigner who came searching to recover his health in this beautiful dry air, and for a Dutchman especially, brought up in the damp of peat ground and the bosom of a polder and city canals, the climate of this northern land of sun remains a source of enjoyment and admiration.

And about what else would I write to you. Do you know a topic that makes more entertaining letters?

Not politics, I hope? Not when you know that one calls the proceedings of the Canadian House of Parliament "la chronique scandaleuse du pays", when you know that no session passes without 'revelation' about mismanagement and dishonesty by ministers and members of Parliament.

No, for a critique about Canadian politics, my pen is too virginal; the columns in your paper are too reputable.

Neither would one wish commentary about the 'spring exhibition' of the 'Art Association of Montreal' that opened yesterday with an evening reception for members and artists. Certainly not, if you had seen those two rooms full of paintings, without a shred of art. They were all plates and prints.

Exhibition Room — Art Gallery, Montreal 1879

I make an exception for "Toiling Homeward" by James L. Graham[75] whose very daring, chunky plough-horses, the one blue-white, the other brown and hairy, masterly expressed the idea of 'toil and slave'.

I bring to your attention this seventeen-year-old as being our animal painter for the future and wish the amiable Brymner[76] luck with such a student.

But for the rest, nothing was worth mentioning for a public that could choose to visit an art exhibition of the present Dutch masters and could visit daily Arti and Scheltema and Holkema and Buffa.[77]

These last two I miss very much here. Montreal is a nice city, but there is no art to see. Other Amsterdammers abroad would miss the Concertgebouw[78] or Volksvlijt[79] or Lucas Bols [bar] or the Beurs; as an old wayfarer, I miss the Kalverstraat and Buffa.

That enjoyable permanent 'display' in front of the showcase, where all classes mingle and jostle to see the new etching of Mesdag or a watercolour by Mauve[80], and the politeness while the people press on, the absence of shouting "Nou, dauw niet zoo", [do not push], after all certainly induced by the unconscious action of the beautiful on one's disposition, that was, for me, typically Amsterdam-like, that I will find nowhere else. No, also in the sphere of the arts, nothing is new in Montreal. What is special at this moment is the strange, amazing season with the lovely weather.

The dry air with such a high electric potential behaves on the lungs like champagne on the imagination, and the strong sunshine, the unclouded sun with its golden rays reflects on the buoyant cold winter earth, which she returns into the delicate air to the pleasure of walking mankind.

This is the ending of winter that has nothing of a winter other than bare trees and the dry grass, or a pre-spring that has only in common with spring the lengthening days and the lovely weather.

We are writing almost in May and there is still not a primrose to see in the scanty grass; the nakedness of the bare gardens is not covered by the colour coat of crocuses and anemones and tulips and the snowdrops which find this snow too high and much too heavy; they do not feel at home here.

But the few plants, which fulfill their Easter duty with their resurrection from the winter death, are therefore doubly welcomed and are very much celebrated.

'Pussy willows', the willow foliage in bud, is often plucked these days and carried by all pedestrians.

By pedestrians, I mean those one meets at Mount Royal — the hill where Montreal works its way upwards, from which she derived her name in the period when Canada was French and was governed by the Jesuits — not the strollers of Sherbrooke and St. Catherine Streets, who decorate themselves with purchased silver stem roses, forgetting the old rule that flowers and kisses must be stolen or given, not bought.

The happy group of pedestrians to which I belong, as often as I have time to, certainly know how to find the scarce flowers and buds on the south side of the hill where the bright sun, the sun of Genoa and Venice, plays so happily with the small single-day rivulets, the mountain streams of melting snow, searching their way through thick and thin, over and under the moss.

Last Sunday I saw the hepaticas already flowering; yet, I did not see them outside in the grass — but guess where — on the pulpit of the Unitarian Church!

One cannot, in fact, call it a pulpit. It is a lectern on an elevated area on which stood a brown Japanese vase, holding a white nosegay and purple hepaticas.

I learned that the young girls of his congregation go out during the last days of the week to ensure that their minister has a bouquet of the earliest flowers of the season on Sunday.

This is a sweet, simple tribute that refined young girls pay to the teacher which they worship profoundly — young girls whose time is very well-filled with domestic, social, philanthropic, (and who knows what other duties), but who in the spring find time every week for a long walk to the sunny spots where the early flowers are.

And now that I have come to know him these days, I understand that Padre W. S. Barnes[81] *inspires worship and affection.*

When one sees him standing in front of his congregation, the well-built powerful man, in the narrow clasp coat with his long grey beard and moustache, the fine straight nose, the high forehead and those, if one is allowed to say, intensely friendly eyes, then one already starts to love him, but one says only what one also says of many a man — a captivating appearance and perhaps he makes you think of Lessing's Patriarch or of the Professor of Israel. But when one hears him! One is soon captured by the charm of the wondrous sound of that most serious and sympathetic voice, full of nuances. His language is well-constructed with emphasis on the Word of God.

And while listening, one realizes that here speaks a scholar and a pious man and an esthetic-sensitive man, apparently unconscious of these three characteristics. He is only conscious of the conviction that mankind has a need for idealism and altruism, and the belief that the religion of Jesus, the Jesus of the synoptic evangelicals, provides that need.

And the stream of his conviction takes you away and one is breathlessly captivated by the fiery sentences which hits the steel of his mind with the flint of his heart, and you feel how the stress of your own facial features gives that small shiver in the neck that I only experience by strong emotions caused by something very beautiful.

His acceptance of the Old Testament critique of Kuenen, Wellhausen and Robertson Smith[82] *made him intolerable to the Presbyterian Church and he linked up with the 'Unitarians', a sect that existed in America already long since, in Canada for almost fifty years. Here, he is completely at home.*

Here, his critical explanation of the Old Testament is valued. On Sundays after church, he holds a short lecture about that topic. While a part of the congregation disperses over Beaverhill, house-mothers take care of the lunch and children who yearn for a play on the open air — because it is, as I said, lovely weather and young and old go outside — obeying the unspoken command "serrez les rangs" and the church benches in front of the church are soon fully occupied.

That is what we did at boarding school on Saturday evenings when the headmaster told one of his beautiful stories and all fifty boys huddled together on the three row-front benches, hanging on his lips and wept, laughed, trembled and cheered, balled their fists or held their breath, depending on the adventures of the hero the story told.

Then we shunned the small corridors between the benches and walked to the front, over desks and tables, so as to lower ourselves with a jump between the touching shoulders of two sitting comrades — a broad wedge of flesh, we are now dignified and composed and walk silently over the soft carpet and shove unobtrusively into the quiet stately benches with a polite nod to the woman who happened to be beside us.

Also, in light of the new critique, the old Israelites remain an interesting people and it is a great pleasure to hear these well-educated scholars discuss the history of the twelve tribes.

Outside the church on Beaverhill (the wide boulevard that leads left to the river toward downtown and the city, to the right of the hill toward the better quarters), the sun burns on the asphalt and on the high sidewalks of the houses. We walk slowly, together with the stream of churchgoers returning home. Cheerful spring dresses give a lot of colour in the bright light.

On the street, the dust is disturbing. On Sundays no sprinkling is done, but sprinkling is necessary in this dry air while the snow is still melting. But on the hill it is lovely and, while walking at noon, I looked at the slow progress of the 'late spring'. I see, close by, a bunch of flowering hepaticas, the small leaves of the primrose veriae spring forth and I already know what will be in the Japanese vase on Sunday in the Unitarian Church.

Former residence of Boissevain, Metcalfe Avenue, Montreal 1993

Prairie greyhounds
(C.P.R. "No. 1," Westbound)

I swing to the sunset land —
The world of prairie, the world of plain,
The world of promise and hope and gain,
The world of gold, and the world of grain,
    And the world of the willing hand.

I carry the brave and bold —
The one who works for the nation's bread,
The one whose past is a thing that's dead,
The one who battles and beats ahead,
    And the one who goes for gold.

I swing to the "Land to Be,"
I am the power that laid its floors,
I am the guide to its western stores,
I am the key to its golden doors,
    That open alone to me.

Emily Pauline Johnson

Chapter Fourteen
Western Canada

After ostensibly linking the east of Canada with the west of Canada, the Canadian Pacific Railway began encouraging immi-gration to Western Canada in earnest. Fortuitously, the International Colonial and Export Trade Exhibition in Amsterdam, held May 1 to October 31, 1883, served as a platform to promote Canada as a land of boundless oppor-tunities. The CPR not only sold tickets for immigrant railway travel, but was also in the business of selling land and providing a unique travel experience to and through the Rockies. Tourism, a relatively new industry for Canada, was expected to become an additional profitable venture. About the same time as the fair was held, the CPR representative for continental Europe, René R. H. toe Laer, surely pioneered in promoting Canada, commencing with the distribution of numerous colourful brochures and leaflets about Canada throughout Europe.[83] It is, of course, impossible to measure the actual impact of toe Laer's marketing efforts on the Dutch public in general. However, the impression left by the CPR's ambitious undertaking possibly enticed a few travellers from the wealthy segment of Dutch society to venture as far as the Canadian West at the end of the 19th century.

It is fortunate that at least four gentlemen who had decided to explore Western Canada also recorded their journeys. Ernst

Sillem, during his world tour from 1888 to 1890, took the CPR from Quebec City to Vancouver. In 1893, Frederik Christiaan Colenbrander took the opportunity to head north from his trip through the USA, via the Dakotas, for a brief tour from Winnipeg to Yorkton, in what is now Saskatchewan. At the end of August in the same year, L. R. J. A. Roosmale Nepveu also arrived in Yorkton via the now-defunct Manitoba and Northwestern Railway. In 1891, Dr. Cornelis Wijnaendts Francken entered Canada at Victoria after travelling through the United States.

René R. H. toe Laer

Toronto to Vancouver, 1888

Ernst Sillem

Ernst Sillem, 1888

Ernst Sillem, a young and well-connected banker from Amsterdam, had travelled via New York and Boston to Canada. During the few days he spent sightseeing in Montreal, he visited the CPR head office where he received free train tickets for his Canada journey, directly from the hands of none other than Cornelius Van Horne[84], the company's president. From there he travelled west, and stayed a few days in Toronto where he was entertained by some of Toronto's prominent people. On his last day there, November 27, 1880, he took a morning drive with the Reverend Arthur Burson[85] in one of Robert Kilgour's carriages and following a dinner with him[86] at the house of Kazimier,[87] he stepped on a late night train on his way to Victoria. From there, he would take a boat to Seattle and continue his journey through the United States, eventually departing from San Francisco toward Yokohama, Japan.

Toronto-Banff, November 28, 1888

"We arrived this morning at 8.30 a.m. at North Bay [Ontario] and because there was no dining car on the train, I had breakfast in a hotel. There was snow everywhere, but there had been a thaw and the roads were treacherous. I purchased a pair of American overshoes. The village counted only a few houses, a school, a church and the rail maintenance yard and workshop.

There were several emigrants on the train. The sleeping cars for the emigrants have no bedding, therefore they use their own mattresses.

At 10 o'clock, the train from Montreal arrived. In the morning, we passed through spruce forests, and toward afternoon we passed large mountains and rocks and many lakes, which were all frozen over. The company in the sleeping car included five gentlemen, five ladies and five children. A young lady travelled by herself from Toronto to Victoria. This is not done in Europe, but here it is accepted.

During the day I did not become acquainted with anyone. My head cold progressed so I lay down on my seat. By the evening however, I was in the smoking room and started to talk with an Englishman, who turned out to be the brother of Fraser who I had met at Lord Radstock's home in London. He is in Canada for business and on his way to Winnipeg. Today I have taken a lot of aconite[88] because I left the homeopathic medicine in my suitcase. Not smart.

On the way to Winnipeg, November 29, 1888

This morning, we pass through very beautiful rocky terrain all times close alongside Lake Superior where the rocks are coloured a fiery red and pink. At Port Arthur, the countryside is not as nice. There are extensive remains of burned-down forests of which one can only see the bare trunks standing and laying along the road. Furthermore, the soil is rocky and not suitable for farming. It seems, however, that there are many mines here located, among which one, is a rich silver mine. At Port Arthur starts a new branch of the CPR, and there one started to use the 24-hour time measure. Therefore, one talks about afternoon as 13 hours, 14 hours, etc.

At Fort William, I saw the largest grain elevator in the world. These are large warehouses where the grain is kept in the top of the building. When it has to be loaded on to a ship, the ship will position itself beside the warehouse and a pipe will be placed from the top of the building to the ship. The grain flows like liquid. Boxcars drive underneath the building and are loaded that same way. Mr. Fraser told me about a financial plan he had developed and also showed it to me. He had also shown it to a couple of CPR gentlemen who had expressed interest in it. I presented them with an introduction to Rudolph [Martinsen].[89]

The train moves now very slowly; the area is rocky and barren.

CPR Elevator, Fort William 1887

Winnipeg–Banff, November 30, 1888

This morning, the terrain became more level and more fertile. We arrived at 12 o'clock in Winnipeg. Mr. Van Horne had given me a letter of introduction addressed to the superintendent there, but he was not at home. His assistant offered one of the employees to show me the city. It is a very new city with broad streets and still only a few large stone buildings.

The air was beautifully fresh and the sun shone clearly. There was thick frost on the trees and telegraph cables. Around Winnipeg, the earth is as flat as a billiard table and fertile.

The assistant superintendent had given orders that the train could not leave before I had returned, but we had a 1 hour and 20 minutes stopover and I did not need more time to see the city.

Fraser stayed in Winnipeg. I had again a very interesting conversation with him and he gave me an introduction to his brother who is at Maclaine & Watson in Batavia.[90]

Several passengers have left and people started to talk more with each other. This evening, I had a conversation with the young lady who travels alone. Her name is Miss Bullen. We ride through extended grain fields, which are regrettably bare.

Winnipeg CPR Station, 1897

Winnipeg–Banff, December 1, 1888

Throughout the whole day, we pass through very dull prairies. Luckily, the passengers started to talk more with each other. An American with his wife and small son had a letter game with which we kept ourselves occupied. That way the morning passed. There is a girl of not even 10 years old on board who travelled with her uncle and aunt, who yesterday evening departed. Their niece was put into care of Miss Bullen. The girl has to go to a place named Medicine Hat, where her father is an officer with the Mounted Police. They are 1,000 men strong and serve to keep the Indians in control and to catch horse thieves, etc. That girl had stayed with her grandparents and had not seen her parents for 2 years.

We passed a station where some Indians had offered buffalo horns for sale. The Indians looked dirty and wore multi-coloured blankets and some carried a child on their back. Their faces were painted red and yellow. These are Cree Indians.

This afternoon I got a sore throat and I was told that the cause was the alkali in the water, which we drank during the last days. An old American lady gave me some potash tablets and now the sore throat is over.

In the evening, I eat in the dining car. That car is hooked up in the morning and left behind at a station for the train that goes eastward. In that way, every dining car has its own section of the route. After dinner, I had again a long conversation with Miss Bullen. At 8.30 p.m., we passed a place where someone wanted to drill a well, but at a depth of 1,800 feet they discovered 'natural gas' instead of water. The gas flows out of a pipe and in the evening it is ignited and a large flame lights the surrounding area.

Banff, Sunday, December 2, 1888

This morning at 5 o'clock the conductor of the sleeping car woke me up. At 5:20 a.m., we arrived in Banff. It was quite cold and pitch-dark, of course. A sledge took me with five other passengers to the CPR Hotel.

I had rested enough and took a bath. The hotel is surrounded by high mountains which are all covered by snow. It is 10 degrees Fahrenheit but it does not feel cold.

I went to the Presbyterian Church where the Rev. McLeod[91] preached. He is very young and preaches very well. After the service, I gave him a letter from Kilgour. He asked me to join a meal at his place, after which he had to preach in the afternoon at a place 5 miles away, and in the evening, at another 10 miles away. He lives with the schoolteacher and has to cook for himself.

I spent two pleasant hours with him. He visits settlements that are located in an area of 200 miles. All of a sudden, the wind started to blow and the temperature started to rise. The temperature now reads 30° F.

In the afternoon I walked to the Cave, a naturally warm sulphurous basin where one can swim. The view of the mountains is sometimes beautiful. In the summer, it is supposed to be even nicer here.

Around six o'clock, I drank tea with the schoolmaster and at nine o'clock, I paid my bill at the hotel and went to bed early, to be able to leave early the following morning. The hotel is very good; one cannot expect to see a better hotel in eastern Canada.

Banff–Vancouver, December 4, 1888

At 4:30 a.m., I was awakened. When I went downstairs at 5:00, there had been a telephone call from the station about a delay of 40 minutes for the train. When I arrived at the station, I had to wait another hour. The reason for the delay was that the water supply pipe in the locomotive was frozen and it took almost two hours to defrost it.

We passed through a beautiful, rugged area straight over the Rocky Mountains. The track is often very narrow and makes very tight turns. Twice, I travelled on the locomotive, which is very well protected and where it felt warmer than cold. There one can see straight ahead very well. A small book that was given to me in Boston at the CPR office contains all kinds of information about places along the track that is very interesting.

The Selkirks, especially, are covered with very thick snow. This was to the salvation of a second-class passenger who fell from a car on the platform and landed in the snow. He got on his feet and followed the train while his friends signalled that the train should be stopped. This incident had a happy ending.

Up in the mountains, wooden shelters are constructed, overhanging the track to prevent the snow from blocking the track.

Banff–Vancouver, December 4, 1888

When I woke up this morning, the train was standing still. I did not see a station anywhere and soon I learned that a landslide had blocked the track. A large pile of snow and soggy soil covered the rails. It rained and the weather was mild. Workers were called in but it took a long time before they arrived. Finally, the time had come and the track was passable again. The delay lasted two hours and 45 minutes.

We followed the Fraser River and noticed beautiful rock formations and high foaming waterfalls. At 9:30 a.m., we arrived at a station for breakfast. Since I understood that we were not on schedule, I had a big breakfast and was therefore able to do without food until 6:30 p.m. We continued along the Fraser, amongst endless pine forests with an Indian village here and there. In the vicinity of Vancouver, the forest still had some nice high trees but many are cut down.

Vancouver Harbour showing tree stumps, 1888-1892

At four o'clock, we arrived and I booked into the CPR Hotel Vancouver. I went to the post office, however to my surprise there was no mail for me.

Vancouver, December 5, 1888

I realize that I had travelled from Banff with the Earl of Listowel, who will go on to Victoria, where his son, Viscount Ennismore[92], has been dangerously ill (Typhus). Right after our train arrived, a steamboat left for Victoria and one hour later, another left for Japan and China. The schedule provided a very short connection.

This morning I mailed several Christmas cards to Holland and a letter to Gudo[93] (my fiancée). At 1:30 p.m., I made riding tour with one of the staff members of the hotel through the park reserved by the government. Very tall and broad pine trees grow there. On one side, it is bordered by English Bay (a gulf of the Pacific Ocean). In one corner of the park were situated a few shacks which housed people with smallpox. This section of the park was put under quarantine by the government so that the Chinese, in particular, would not come into contact with the sick and spread the illness. In the middle of the park, we came upon a fence and we had no other choice than to return along the same pathway. However, I had already seen the nicest part.

In July 1866, the city of Vancouver had burned down leaving only one house standing. It once again has between 9,000 and 10,000 inhabitants. Everything was rebuilt so quickly that between the houses the stumps of the cut-down trees are still in the ground. The large trees are cut down at a man's height. They dig a hole in the bottom of trunk and light a fire in it. That way the trunk and the roots at a certain depth carbonize and one can cut down the remains more easily. Sometimes they use dynamite.

This is a city in which one can make money. If I did not have a job, then I would for certain settle here in search of my fortune!

The Hotel Vancouver is very good. I find the CPR hotels the best I have ever seen. The food and the service are first-rate and everything is tidy. Also the trains are lovely and well-furnished, better than in the United States, and the rails lie flush.

The cafeterias where one has breakfast or lunch are excellent and even cheaper than in the United States.

I noticed that there are only four first-class passengers on the boat to Japan and also 150 Chinese who returned to China with the money they had earned. I am glad that I do not travel with that shipping line. I wrote to Gudo this evening.

Vancouver–Victoria, December 6, 1888

Firstly, I repacked and sorted my suitcases. Afterward, I purchased a couple of photos of Vancouver and the road between Banff and here.

At 2:30 p.m. the steamer Yosemite *departed for Victoria on Vancouver Island, where I arrived at 8:30 p.m. They navigate quite closely to the coast the entire time. The water was very calm. This ship is the only one that maintains a service between Vancouver and Victoria, and is owned by the CPR. She delivers daily, except Mondays, the travellers from Victoria in time for the train to the east and departs again after the arrival of that train.*

Victoria, December 7, 1888

First thing this morning, I took the introduction letter from Mr. Kilgour to Mr. Thomas Henderson[94]. He asked me to have supper with him at his house. On my way, I took out some money so that I have enough until San Francisco.

I had inquired where Mr. Bullen[95] *lived and after lunch I walked to his place. It was half-way between Victoria and Esquimalt. I found Miss Bullen and met her sister-in-law, whose daughter was suffering from scarlet fever. They asked me whether I was afraid about it, but I was already in the house and let it take its course. They invited me for dinner on Sunday but I told them that tomorrow I would be going on. I walked back to the hotel, and at 6 o'clock went to Mr. Henderson's, where I drank tea and dined with him and his wife. Today, it rained a large part of the day.*

Victoria, December 8, 1888

At nine o'clock a.m., I went again to see Henderson and, after I bought my ticket for Portland, we drove together through the city and its surroundings.

It rained off and on but we were still able to leave the carriage open for most of the time. The ride went along the bay called English Bay and through a nature park of which many are here. It was very nice, but too foggy to see across the bay. We did see a few steamboats arrive. The harbour of Victoria is very suitable for shipping and well-sheltered. Close by is the harbour of Esquimalt which must be the nicest harbour of the world, where the whole British navy could be safely moored.

Esquimalt Harbour, circa 1900

A few moored ships were being loaded, among them the Viola, which was being loaded with crates filled with canned salmon bound for Liverpool. The salmon was shipped in by a steamboat from New Westminster, a town located on the Fraser River. There are large factories where the salmon is preserved. The rivers here must be full of salmon. At 11 o'clock, the boat left by which I will travel to Tacoma where I will catch a train for Portland. Henderson escorted me on board.

It is beautiful saloon-paddle-steamer. At first the weather was good, but later on it rained heavily again. We entered Puget Sound and stopped in Port Townsend, a small harbour, from where a lot of lumber is shipped. There were five sailing ships docked. The hilly shores are richly wooded.

In Seattle at 7 o'clock, I transferred to another boat, which would later arrive at 9 o'clock in Tacoma, from where I would then take a train to Portland."

Manitoba and Saskatchewan, 1893

Frederik Christiaan Colenbrander

The following excerpts of letters from Canada to Netherlands were written by Frederik ('Frits') Christiaan Colenbrander about the Canadian leg of his orientation tour. Attracted specifically by the World Exhibition in Chicago, he made his way to North America in 1893. Colenbrander, belonging to a well-to-do family, together with his two blue-blooded companions, Godfried Leonard ('Go') Baron van Boetzelaer[96] and Conrad ('Coen') Jonkheer van de Merwede Quarles van Ufford[97] departed on Saturday, June 3, 1893, aboard the Spaarndam, N.A.S.M.[98] from Rotterdam. With Captain Frederik H. Bonjer keeping an eye on the bridge, all three men, who were from privileged backgrounds, sailed in luxurious First-Class accommodations across the Atlantic "having an unprecedented good table". After arriving in New York, they would start their journey with a briefcase full of letters of introduction that took them first to Niagara Falls, N.Y, then to Chicago, Illinois and Orange City, Iowa where they would part company with Quarles van Ufford. From there, Colenbrander and van Boetzelaer travelled via St. Paul, Minnesota to Jamestown, North Dakota where they visited Messrs. Knuppe[99] and Hartsinck[100] who were representatives of the Netherlands-America Land Company. While in Jamestown, Colenbrander wrote:

"I had half a mind to go north once to Manitoba where Uncle Leembruggen's[101] immigrants are going. We are close by and it would be a good opportunity. And it is also not too much off course to go from there to California, San Francisco and Yellowstone Park".

Frederik Christiaan Colenbrander

On July 23, 1893, Colenbrander wrote to his mother from Winnipeg where he had arrived at 2:30 p.m. from St. Paul, Minnesota via Jamestown and Grand-Forks, North Dakota:

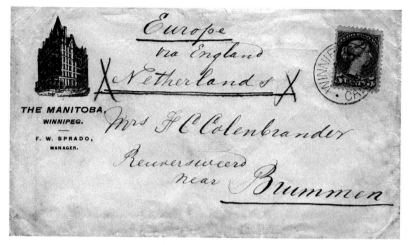

Manitoba Hotel envelope, cancelled Winnipeg, July 24, 1893

"After the inspection of our baggage, we went to our hotel[102] *[The Manitoba], and so, there we were in Canada. Because of all kinds of little things, one immediately notices that one is in an English world. I cannot say that it is unpleasant, however today was very boring because everything was closed like a lid on a pot. This morning we visited the Anglican Church, which was not as I expected. First a litany of singing, a ceremonious hum for about an hour, after that a superficial sermon of about 26 minutes, and that was all.*

Winnipeg is still young, which you noticeable in just about everything. It has 30,000 inhabitants. Our plan for tomorrow is to go from here to Portage la Prairie and then from there to Yorkton, where Nepveu[103] *and Insinger*[104] *live. Mr. Hartsinck knew both gentlemen and wrote to them that we were coming. It must however be a backward area and I don't know how to get there, as yet. Timetables are rare here. Each line has its own timetable and just simply ignores all the other ones. So far as I know, there is* not a train everyday*, and on Sunday everything is closed, offices and stores, so we could not get any information. In any event, it will be a trip of no less than* *ten hours. It was, fortunately, cooler today, but still 86 degrees in the shade. The evenings are always cool, sometimes even cold. We had first thought that we would go to see Yellowstone Park on our way to San Francisco, as soon as possible, after we had seen enough of this place (and we don't think we will stay very long)."*

Colenbrander and van Boetzelaer travel on from Winnipeg to Portage la Prairie where they will stay a short while, and from where he also writes the following letter to his sister.

Albion Hotel, Portage la Prairie, July 26, 1893

Dear Jek[105],

As a variation on the theme, I am writing to you and now thanking you right away for your letters. I cannot answer each of them separately because we have not had enough time. Sunday afternoon, I wrote to Mother thinking that the letter would arrive about August 5. I wish all of you the best again with the good fortune of being together in health and happiness at the [birthday] party. Perhaps those two letters will arrive at the same time. Anyway, congratulate Mamma very much for me again, and convey my kisses to Mamma as a sign of my best wishes for her and all our happiness.

You know that we are in Winnipeg! We think we will start by going to Yorkton, the residence of the gentlemen Nepveu and Insinger, and the place where uncle Henk's[106] *immigrants went. I had written to you earlier that we were curious about the right means of transport. Monday morning (when the offices and stores were open again), our first job was to ask how we could get there.*

We had gone to the ticket office of the Manitoba and North-Western Railway Company because, you should know, it is the custom here (at least in the cities) to buy train tickets in the city, and not at the station. Every company has a large ticket office in the city. There we learned the following: Namely, that Yorkton is, for now, the end point of the Manitoba and North-Western Railway line, actually a recently-built branch line which is bit-by-bit extended further while the company is truly focused on selling its land holdings in concert with the extension of the line. The problem was, however, that on [the Northern Branch], which is the only one to reach that place, a train goes only every other day. It was very disappointing to know that the first train, which went on Tuesday, yesterday, did not continue to Yorkton, so we would have to wait until Thursday. Imagine hearing on Monday that the first train goes Thursday! First we thought to cancel the journey, but since we had come so far, that would be crazy. To plan this in advance was impossible, since, you understand, that timetables from busy railroads as far away as Fargo in North Dakota are not available, so we did not have to blame ourselves for carelessness or hastiness. In order not to lose time until Thursday, we travelled ahead with another train to Portage la Prairie, where we are now. Portage is not a big city. It is, again, a very new town of about 4,000 inhabitants. We had no clue about where to go in this town when we arrived here yesterday, because in Winnipeg they could not give us a good hotel address. Of course the result was that we ended up in a very bad hotel, at first. Soon afterward, we found something better, where we are now, and I think that this is the best hotel in the city. The rooms here are at least clean and tidy; imagine, this is in a wooden building, which is surprisingly neatly built and finished. In such a wooden building, I am mostly concerned about fire, however, one has electric light, of course, which is very reassuring.

Arriving at an American hotel is very strange. At the station, one gets into a bus for which one pays 25 cents per person on arrival, because the [horse-drawn] bus is never run by the hotel but by a hired coachman. Upon arrival, the first thing is to write your name in a book and then they ask if you want a room. If so, then the clerk writes the room number behind your name and you can go and eat or look at your room.

In short, that is it. When we arrived at the first hotel, right away I found it dubious and the rooms dirty. Well, then we left our baggage, did not say anything, and went again into the city. One can just walk into a hotel, no one says or asks you anything, if you don't say anything.

The [Albion Hotel][107] seemed to us the best-looking from the front desk. They again asked our names, rooms were tidy, very neat and clean, with clean linens. All being fine, we simply had our hand luggage brought from the other hotel without needing to go there *ourselves. That is the way one operates in America, without wasting time with talking. Our board cost $1.50 per day. There are set hours for meals: breakfast from 6:30 to 9:30, dinner from 12:00 to 2:00, supper from 6:00 to 8:00. One has to be sure to be on time, or, all of a sudden, the door closes and then one has to see how to get something in a lunchroom in the city.*

Albion Hotel, Portage la Prairie, Manitoba

Yesterday afternoon, Go and I drove west of the city and saw many farms, planted for the most part with good grain, almost all of them in wheat, oats or grassland. Many farms are built shabbily, log houses built from wood logs placed one on top of the other and not like other houses made with planks. They can, therefore, be just as good and cozy and perhaps even better, however, not as nice or striking to look at. For example, for a newcomer, a church and a rectory made of wood logs appears somewhat strange, at first.

Whenever one nears a small river or creek one finds trees and shrubs. That is, if one sees some bush from a distance one can almost be certain that there is a river. Unfortunately, it usually teems with mosquitoes — so bad that one unavoidably gets bitten everywhere, constantly slapping and scratching to keep them away from your body.

Yesterday evening, we went to a musical performance by a young lady, namely Miss Miller, who must have been born here. Actually, for a place like this, it was quite interesting. In a small amusement hall, the singing of Miss [Edith] Miller[108] and participating gents was, of course, very reedy. In any event, one is very content if something like that can been found in a town like this. Perhaps, this afternoon, we will drive to the other side and, tomorrow morning, we will go on the Thursday train to Yorkton. Nepveu and Insinger live some distance away from there. If we do not get away before Monday, the next opportunity is Friday. If that were to be the case, then our plan would be to first return to Winnipeg and then to go from there, with the shortest possible delay, to Yellowstone National Park, a journey of two and one-half days on the train.

I am afraid that I cannot write in the coming days but, in any case, I shall still write before we go to the true far West, that is, before Monday or Tuesday. Go and I are perfectly healthy and I hope that you all are also all right. It always makes me feel good to hear how everyone is doing. Many, many greetings to Mama, Papa, Uncle B., family B., Aunt P., Grandfather, the aunts, the uncles, nephews and nieces in Brummen, Zutphen or wherever they may be. My apologies to Aunt H. that I cannot write because there is really not enough time. Pico and Henri V. wrote to me and I have not been able to answer them yet. And now, Jek and other family branches, I have nothing more to say, so I won't start a new sheet. Hoping to hear from you soon... your loving Frederick. Of course, many greetings to everybody at Reuversweerd[109] and the friends you might meet in the meantime ... Keep up the good spirits!

After having travelled to the Yorkton area where they visited Henri Roosemale Nepveu, Frederik Insinger and some of the Dutch immigrants, Colenbrander and Van Boetzelaer returned by train to Winnipeg, from where the next letter was written.

Winnipeg, August 1, 1893

Dear Parents!

Yesterday evening we returned from our journey to Yorkton and are back in [Winnipeg], from where we think we will depart tomorrow. I wrote my previous letter to Jek from Portage la Prairie, which you surely have received and, thereby, already have learned about our first impressions of Canada. Now, I will tell you about the course of our journey. Beforehand, I will let you know that we both are healthy, despite the tiring travels. We are still alert and in high spirits, especially since we have, in some way, returned to the civilized world. I start, therefore, from Portage la Prairie. We departed from there on Thursday morning, July 17, and we arrived late evening in Yorkton. The trip was long and the slow train was loaded with many passengers because only two trains run each week. On the train, I had a conversation with a Mr. Seeman[110], a man who owns a large amount of land out there, which he initially took over from the Railway Company, to which he had loaned a large amount of money. Now he sells this land for $3 an acre. He then went there to settle. Before this, I think he lived in London or wherever. In short, I asked him about Mr. Insinger, who was well-known there, because he was "something like" a Member of the Legislative Assembly of the Northwest Territories. I also asked him about the Dutch colonists. He did not know much about them and thought that most of the 'Hollanders' had left. This was disappointing to hear, however, later on, this turned out not to be true.

Yorkton is a village with about 30 small houses. The hotel, given the nature of the village, was reasonably good. However, we had the pleasure of encountering bedbugs for the first time there. Luckily, it was only one and it came from another room, where it was known they were already there. People seem not to care, as bedbugs are not the real problem. To explain, they would rather have bedbugs than moths,

Yorkton 1896, showing the Royal Hotel, on the right

because they are all over here. Anyway, Go and I were very cautious, kept everything separated and put a few things in the wash. Thank God we did not find a thing.

The next morning our first job was to hire a carriage and to drive to Mister Nepveu who lived closer than Insinger. The road was easy to find even though there were only a few houses around. The distance was eight miles so it took a little less than two-and-one-half hours. About halfway, we came upon a settlement of the first group of immigrants recruited by the Committee. There were three families who lived together at no cost in a small house with a large piece of land owned by Nepveu's brother-in-law. It was not yet decided where they would finally settle. They were the families de Vries, Heeres and Kamminga.[111] They had worked very hard and, as a result, had nice plants in the field. As a test, they had planted and seeded many different Dutch plants, which turned out more or less successfully. There had been night-frost for a couple of nights, which had severely damaged the beans and potatoes — the latter, however, less severely.

The people were very satisfied and especially praised the kindness and help they received from Nepveu. After we had spent enough time there, we drove to Mr. Nepveu, whom we found at home and who had already heard from Mr. Hartsinck about our visit. We noticed that his wife, a simple person who has never been away from the prairie other than on her journey last spring to Holland, is good-natured and naive. There was also young Bentinck[112] and a certain Sillevis[113], a young man from Leiden, who had just come by to see whether life was attractive enough in order to settle there.

Nepveu lives in a large log house and manages a large number of horses that just run wild there; they drink close to the house and stand around the fire that is built to manage the mosquitoes. The animals hang about, standing in the smoke to escape from those insects. Yes — you have no idea what a plague they are. They are big, nasty mosquitoes that bite viciously and are present in huge numbers, especially near water or wood, for that matter everywhere. Some people wear a veil in front of their face but that's very hot. Go and I were terribly afflicted, but, fortunately enough, with screens one can keep them out of the houses reasonably well.

We stayed the whole day and helped in the afternoon with haying (because those three gentleman do everything together) and I did handle the hayfork. The next day, we drove to Mr. Insinger's, 22 miles to the west. It required more than two-and-one-half hours driving, and was about 12 to 14 miles after passing the last house. You can imagine how isolated he is and how darn careful we had to be in finding our way. Fortuitously, we met Mr. Insinger on our way, not far from his home. We introduced ourselves, however he had to leave urgently (he is almost always gone) and would wait for us in Yorkton. He gave us a note for his foreman, who would show us everything.

We continued to his house and were to finally leave there in the evening. This was also a very primitive log house with numerous stables and roughly-made sheds, where he holds his yearling horses in the winter. In summer, however, everything runs loose outside. Mr. Insinger also has a so-called horse ranch and does nothing other than breeding horses.

He has a large herd, of all kinds, mostly light mares, which he then crosses with an English Shire stallion. I did not care much for that stallion. However, he wins trophies and is thereby 'one eye in the land of the blind'. The same can be said for one of Nepveu's — a Clydesdale, nothing special, but it does not matter here. I do not believe that the horse business is very lucrative. However, it must have been fairly good and it does not involve too much work. The only thing that one has to do is to mow a lot of grass in the summer which dries in one or two days, and then to move it from the field and stack it up for the winter.

Workhorses and cattle never see grass or hay and that is why those farms or ranches are located so far from each other, firstly, to have enough land for grazing and secondly, because there is not enough good grass around. They consider it "good", but I would say that it is only said to be so. However, what I do see is that animals seem to be in foal. Only foals and workhorses sometimes get oats that Mr. Insinger buys from the farmers. Nepveu has grown oats for the first time but good grassland is not always good farmland. About an hour from Insinger's house, we visited de Vries and other immigrants, [Rienstra], Verhaag, Broersma and Kalsbeek[114] who had arrived about fourteen days ago and were building a log house. This of course did not go easily, since none of them is a carpenter. However, it does not take much architectural training, so they will manage. Their wives were still in the immigrants' shed in Yorkton. They had two oxen teams, three cows, a wagon and they were very busy and seemed to be in good spirits.

In the evening, we arrived in town again. Mr. Insinger arrived after 12 o'clock at night and we met him the next morning. He was already very busy. He is an odd kind of man, restless always, away on business, mostly for government affairs. He was born in Brummen, however I believe he left the town at the age of two and hence did not remember anything about it. In the afternoon, he drove us to a farm close by, occupied by a certain Mr. Bull. I have never seen such lovely oats and wheat, never or nowhere, a sign that there is good land. Bull arrived there poor, nine years ago and is now well-off.

There we also talked with Klaas de Vries,[115] one of the two brothers who had arrived two years ago along with Mr. Insinger, and who often writes letters, some of which are printed in Het Lampje,[116] *amongst other publications. He was very satisfied and told us he would be able to start farming for himself in about three years. Presently, he is a farmhand earning $200 a year and kept in contact with his brother and mother in Holland. He wanted his mother to come over. That is quite nice. However, it seems difficult to find work here. There are only a few settlers and everybody looks after themselves as much as is possible.*

This evening, after Mr. Insinger had driven home, we had to wait until 12 o'clock in the evening before there was a train. During that time we drove to Nepveu to say goodbye. They welcomed us very warmly. So, in looking at it, I would get on better with N. than Ins.

My opinion about the country has changed for the better. I believe one can do very well, in the good areas, of course. This land is not ready for making profits from land speculation by a long shot, especially because the land is cheap and one can get land for free as homesteads from the state. However, I believe this is a good land for poor colonists. Of course, for the first years they have to struggle and work hard, nevertheless, one can grow beautiful wheat. The winters are terribly cold (last year, minus 56 degrees) and sometimes the harvest freezes. I do not think that the businesses of Mr. I. nor Mr. N. are profitable.

We departed Sunday evening at 12 o'clock and arrived in Winnipeg at 5:30 p.m. Wonderful to be at a tidy hotel again! A bath did a lot of good. In the back lands, the American seems to think that one can wash oneself with a drop of water and dry with a hanky, considering the way the hotels are furnished.

Today, Tuesday, we were very busy. First, we received many letters from all of you — therefore many thanks — and also letters forwarded from Mr. Hartsinck. We wired him and Hospers to send mail to the Main North Hotel, Hotsprings, Yellowstone and we had to write both gentlemen to explain the wire and to thank Mr. Hartsinck for his efforts. We first had to make a tour de force to get our tickets, which we purchased for the low price of $25.00. I had to get money at the bank again, since I cannot get any before we arrive at San Francisco or Portland. So, I exchanged three notes of 10 pounds sterling each, and received $4.80 per pound sterling, a total of $144.00. Tomorrow, I will again have to exchange the remaining into American dollars because, in the States, Canadian dollars are not accepted. I told the bank this and they promised to do it without charging extra fees.

Furthermore, I had my clothing repaired, did some shopping, such as for a bit of tobacco, etc., for the long trip. Before one knows it, the day is over. Cleaning clothes and underwear also took a long time, as we were thickly covered with dust.

Dear folks, now I will stop again. I hope soon to have the opportunity to write from Livingstone or from somewhere in

Yellowstone Park. Address your letters for now to Hospers,[117] Orange City. I am always pleased and happy to hear how well you are all doing. May this continue! Thank God, we are, too. Does it rain enough in Europe? Here we had only a bit. Last week while on the train, there was a hail and thunderstorm such as I had never before experienced. The train came to a halt while it was going on. In a quarter of an hour, six inches of hail came down... brrr!! Terrible! I do not think that the crop was much damaged, that is a wonder. And now, again, farewell. We will depart tomorrow at 11:15 a.m. There is still a lot to do. We just received our clean laundry. That means a lot of packing tonight! To each and everyone, I send my best greetings. All live healthy and happy and believe in me.

I had almost forgotten to thank you for the nice drawing. Now I know how I have to dress myself when I am back in Holland. Here, one also sees crazy things and, in general, the American loves to be dressed nicely. This is more pronounced in the eastern parts.

Dear Mother, receive a loving kiss, and to everyone, many compliments from Go.

Your affectionate son, Frederik Jr.

Both gentlemen continued their tour with stops in Yellowstone Park; Butte, Montana; San Francisco, California; Los Angeles, California; Chicago, Illinois; St. Louis, Missouri and New York, N.Y. On October 14, they returned home via Rotterdam, having sailed on the *Veendam*, N.A.S.M., from New York.

134

Saskatchewan, 1893

Lodewijk Reinier Jan Anthonie Roosmale Nepveu

Lodewijk Reinier Jan Anthonie Roosmale Nepveu

On August 31, Roosmale Nepveu and his cousin, Jacob J. Baron Fagel[118], arrived in Yorkton to visit his son, Henri, and Henri's wife, Katharine, and a number of other new Dutch immigrants. L. R. J. A. Roosmale Nepveu was very much involved in Evangelical movements. Among other things, he was one of the founders of the Vereeniging tot Colportage en Evangelisatie (The Organization of Canvassing [selling bibles] and Evangelism) in the three northern provinces of the Netherlands.[119] He also served as one of the members of the Immigration Committee responsible for organizing the first Dutch group immigration to Canada, in April of 1893. This committee was composed of members of the Dutch elite and others with an Orthodox Protestant background. He referred to the immigrants upon meeting with them that they are "good, honest, God-fearing people, but ill-suited to becoming pioneers in a new community."

He goes on to comment on the surroundings.

"It is a strange life, here on the prairies. It is devoid of all wealth and decorum. One cannot observe any difference in social standing. Cultivated young girls work on the land, milk cows, and so on. Just now, I went on horseback to see de Vries, [Klaas or Reindert, a Dutch immigrant] and on my way back I got lost. It is a big exception to encounter anyone. However, my horse knew the way home, and brought me back again. Afterwards we bridled a wild horse that is to bring us to see the other Dutchmen tomorrow. My son [Henri] was allowed to catch it with a lasso. When I wanted to climb onto the wagon, it jumped so high and made such a commotion that I fell off it backwards.

Every once in a while, my son and Cousin Fagel shoot prairie chickens, a kind of partridge but a little bigger, which in abundance here and are very tame. They are very tasty!

On the prairies, you can find all sorts of flowers and an abundance of wild fruits that are delicious to eat. The harvest turned out to be very good, especially the hay. Wheat suffered by a kind of mice (larger than rats, however) called gophers. There are a great many of them, and they are very destructive. There are also a great many prairie fires. We passed one on the train. It was immense.It is very warm here, but the nights are cool. You never see a cloud in the sky. It is clearly noticeable that this is a different climate, and a much more cheerful one than ours. One does not suffer much from the cold, but also less from the great heat. I am covered with bites from mosquitoes (a sort of gnat), but now there are only a few around. Their time is over. They must have been a real plague earlier in the summer.

A few years of life on the prairies would be good training for many of the young people of our higher classes. Opulence and comfort are entirely absent here. All is plain to the utmost. There is very little chance to obtain service, but the words 'help yourself!' are brought into practice. One learns, nolens volens, to lend a hand, and without any doubt it is a very healthy and invigorating way of life. One is very safe here; one can sleep with the door open. The Indians here are very peaceful. They are no longer numerous; I think that there are only 20,000 in the whole of Canada. With great interest, I noticed near Regina a Christian Missionary School for Indian children.[120] The various denominations have set up such schools here. This one was founded by the Presbyterians.

Regina Indian Industrial School, 1891-1910

As I wrote you on my postcard, the Minister of the Interior[121] has invited me to visit him in Ottawa on my return journey. He first offered to come to see me in Montreal, but I did not dare to accept. Although it will take another two days, I think it is too important not to make the trip to Ottawa.

Both gentlemen followed this visit with a trip to meet with Dutch immigrants in Harrison, South Dakota and then onward to Chicago for the World's Fair.

Victoria to Banff, 1891

Dr. Cornelis Wijnaendts Francken

Dr. Cornelis
Wijnaendts Francken

In 1891, Dr. Cornelis Wijnaendts Francken toured the United States and Canada. Originally trained as a biologist and later having studied psychology and sociology, he became a prolific writer and travelled extensively throughout his life. Being curious about America, he decided to visit a friend in San Francisco and further explore the western part of the continent which, as he stated, was less influenced by Europe, developing freely and independently. He had heard so many good things about the CPR that he decided to make a visit to Canada. From Tacoma, Washington, he went by boat to Victoria, British Columbia and then on to Vancouver, from which he took a train through the Rockies to the Banff Springs Hotel.

"Whereas it was my plan, during my journey through America, to also see the Yellowstone Park, I decided to return from the west coast by the Northern Pacific Railroad toward the east. But I had also heard so many good things about the Canadian Pacific Railroad that I could not refrain from also travelling on the nicest part of that line, and to make a week-long excursion to Banff from Tacoma.

When I now look back on that journey, I really do not regret having also included English possessions in the west during my wanderings; rarely does a tourist get to see so much beauty in a few days for a rather petty price.

British North America, the Dominion of Canada, is the largest overseas possession of the English Crown, even larger than Australia. The largest part, namely 5/7 of the complete surface, the so-called Northwest Territory, is still as yet unpopulated with fewer people than Siberia. The only somewhat populated areas are Quebec and Ontario, where the largest cities are located, amongst which Montreal is the largest, by far.

[Montreal] is for Canada like New York is for the United States and if one wants to draw other similar parallels, then one could probably compare Toronto with Boston, Ottawa with Washington and Winnipeg with Chicago.[122] *The political capital is Ottawa, located exactly on the boundary of the French- and English-speaking population which is the reason, therefore, in 1858, it was elevated to be the capital, after Kingston, Montreal, Quebec and Toronto had successively been the seats of the government.*

As everyone knows, Canada was at the Peace of Paris on February 10, 1783, handed over by France to England after a lengthy war. Presently the British possession in North America is divided up in the following provinces from east to west:

	NAME	CAPITAL
ATLANTIC PROVINCES	Prince Edward Island	Charlottetown
	Nova Scotia	Halifax
	New Brunswick	Fredericton
CENTRAL PROVINCES	Quebec	Quebec
	Ontario	Toronto
	Manitoba	Winnipeg
WESTERN PROVINCES	Athabasca	
	North West Territory	
	Saskatchewan	Regina
	Assiniboia	
	Alberta	
PACIFIC PROVINCE	British Columbia	Victoria

Perhaps one will miss in this list Newfoundland; but this large island, however located close to Canada, nevertheless, does not belong to it, but is a separate crown possession, under which Labrador is also included.

Canada is located considerably closer to the English harbours than New York; the distance from Quebec to Liverpool amounts to 2,645 nautical miles, as opposed to New York to Liverpool, 3,095.

Besides from Quebec over the wide St. Lawrence River, Montreal is also reachable from Halifax by the Intercolonial Railway (850 English miles).

Until recently, it was difficult to penetrate through English territory to the West. In 1870, [Colonel Garnet Wolseley, later Field Marshall Viscount Wolseley], with a small army, needed 95 days to get from Toronto to Winnipeg, a distance that one, now that the railway has been completed, covers in not even two days. The need for a speedier connection was strongly expressed here and already in 1867 it was decided, for military and political motives at a conference of the British American provinces, to build a Pacific Railway. But it was not until 1875 when the work started and in the first years there was not much progress. In 1880, to the satisfaction of the public, further building of it was left to a private company. By this time the commercial advantage was evident, and a year later the Canadian Pacific Railway was already built. The company had made a commitment to the government to finish the work within ten years and received in return a subsidy of 25 million dollars and 25 million acres of land. With great speed, it was worked so hard that across the open plains west of Winnipeg, an average of more than three English miles were laid daily and, on November 7, 1885 at Craigellachie, the last spike could already be inserted. That is why the company, not yet five years old, already had at the end of the year (including the branch lines) 4,315 English miles of rail. That the line, which cost 140 million, was viable became clear from the revenues, which amounted last year (1890) to 16½ million dollars with a positive balance of 6¼ million.

The main line of 2,906 English miles is entirely located on British territory and runs through still unknown areas, which, in my opinion, provides a great future. In relation to the soil, the various areas provide quite different products. It seems to me that one can distinguish mainly five areas from the east to the west successively: central Canada being the government and commercial centre; Ontario, the area above the large fresh water lakes with a lot of timber; Manitoba, an area with many rivers and small lakes and with a large amount of farmland, where a number of grain farmers have settled; Assiniboia and Alberta, prairie plains with lot of cattle and wildlife (water birds, prairie poultry and antelopes), a good country for sportsmen; British Columbia, the mountainous areas with coal and metal ore mines and a lot of fish, mainly salmon in large quantities that is sent to the east, fresh in ice or conserved in cans.

Let's look now a little closer at the three last named provinces, which are still less known for their great importance for the future. We start, therefore, in reverse order, with British Columbia. Because of the closeness of the ocean and being bordered on the east by the high mountain ridge of the Rocky Mountains, there is ample rainfall and is the climate very equable. On Vancouver Island, for example, the temperature never drops below the freezing point and the mercury never rises above 84° F.

The land is very rich with vast forests and therefore supplies quite a lot of good lumber, particular Douglas fir (Abies Douglasii), which has the great value that it does not shrink and can be used green, right away, and why it is also sought after for railway construction. Other industry includes the development of coal, iron and gold and, also, the trade in furs is rather considerable. An important source of income is provided by the fabulous richness in fish. In the first place, there is salmon (notwithstanding that it is already the main food of the population). In 1885, nearly two million pieces weighing more then seven million pounds (3 million kilos) was exported in cans for the value of approximately 900,000 dollars. Besides this, one finds the oolichan, a small fish so rich in oil that in a dry form the Indians burn them as tallow candles. Furthermore, there is herring, halibut, cod and sturgeon, etc. Mainly, these are caught by Indians who still are involved with catching fish often using very primitive tools.

At the eastern slope of the Rocky Mountains, an enormous area of grassland stretches out where Calgary is the prominent town. A good cowboy can make 10 dollars a month here and save from that a pretty penny, especially since he has no opportunity to spend his money for miles on strong spirits. If this would not have been the case, then Calgary (and other towns along the railway) while now being a quiet and orderly city, would most likely have been made up of a rowdy population of wranglers, just like in the new cities in the west of the US, with their many saloons that many times cause scenes of dangerous drunkenness. However, something like that is impossible here because almost nowhere on earth is there a larger movement going for the abolishment of, and abstinence from, alcoholic beverages (temperance movement) than in Canada, with the fortunate result that ten times less per head is used there than in England.

Calgary 1890, showing Eau Claire Mill (extreme right)

A distance farther on this large plain is Regina. The headquarters of the North-West Mounted Police is located here. They were established for protection against the predatory Indians, are about 1,000 men strong and have an excellent reputation. Only a few years ago, they quelled the rebellion of Louis Riel, a French half-breed who, since 1870, had led the Métis population in its revolutionary uprising and was later arrested and went to the scaffold in Regina on November 6, 1885.[123]

We must stand still a little longer at Manitoba. The winter starts here in October and lasts five months. Although the cold is very severe, because of the clearness and dryness of the air the low temperature is very easy to endure and the climate is healthy. The work season runs from March until September. The farmlands are here very spacious so that the furrows are an hour long. An example of such a giant farm is the Bell-Farm,[124] which is no less famous than the well-known Dalrymple farm near Fargo. While the latter already covers 55,000 acres, it is still surpassed by the former that covers 64,000 acres (that is about 100 English square miles) and, therefore, is the largest in the world.

Major William R. Bell's farm house 1884

If the furrows were arranged in one single line, it could circle around the earth almost six times. This gigantic piece of farmland belongs to a company but there is a plan, after its development, to divide it and sell it as 250 separate farms. It is understandable that by such dimensions the land is as much as possible being treated with the use of the latest inventions. In general, for example, self-binders are in use, which also bind together the cut grain and, all over, the threshed grain is piled up in towering elevators or grain silos for later shipping. The harvests are rich and of good quality; the acre normally yields 30 or 40 bushels (800–1,100 kilograms) at a value of approximately 30 dollars. Farm hands can, apart from boarding and lodging, earn 50–60 dollars yearly, of which they can put aside 20–35 dollars and can buy their own land within a few years. The purchase conditions are such that if one chooses, one has only 1/10 of the total sum to pay with the remainder to be paid over the next 9 years at 6 % interest per year.

The area is, therefore, very suitable for immigrants but a requirement is that they originally be farmers and not ill-fated salesmen or office clerks. It is much better to come here without any capital but with a sound knowledge of the trade, than with capital but knowing nothing about farming and to having to start to do it from scratch. Up until now, I have consistently withheld my opinions about finance and economics. I also want to do that in this case, except for the satisfied and the positive judgments of the farmers, who had settled in Manitoba and who are mostly Scots, Swedes and Canadians from Ontario. For the moment, let a few of them speak for themselves: "This is the healthiest climate in the world and I consider the future of this country as a success, for certain." "People who want to work have a very good opportunity for prosperity in Manitoba," one judges. Another writes, "I have felt completely content in this land. I could not wish for any better farming and want only that hundreds of farmers in Europe would know this". Add to this the testimony of an authority like Mr. Sandison, a Scot, settled here since 1883 and now one of the largest and richest farmers. He says, in a letter of October 13, 1890, among other things, the following: "There is no reason why a diligent young person with some practical experience in farming would not succeed here. A good worker can expect in a few years good results and does not have to be afraid for the future, when he knows his profession and is willing to work with the requisite intellect and to roll up his sleeves. No one who is competent and willing to work has to hesitate to move to Manitoba."

Finally, let's hear how a completely different man, Mister M.S. Caine, member of the English Parliament who visited these areas in 1887 expressed himself: "In case the British Government, instead of investing money in the doubtful politics of the Irish land purchase, wanted to spend 20 million to gradually transfer 200,000 families of Irish tenant farmers out of the overpopulated districts to Manitoba, then it would be no difficulty to get the money back in small installments from the prosperous farmers that it would create that way. I am surprised why a rich country like England endures the misery of the over-crowded Irish districts, and why it does not transfer a few million of its starving population into the middle of abundance and satisfaction, with the assurance of being paid back every nickel spent."

The extensive and rich resources of Manitoba are reflected in the size and façade of its capital city. It is located at the mouth of the Assiniboine on the Red River, precisely halfway between both oceans. Twenty years ago there was nothing to find here other than a small border crossing at Fort Garry, a trading post of the Hudson's Bay Company with 200 residents. And now emerges, as an important railway centre, a large modern city of 30,000 souls.

Let's return to the Canadian Pacific. Notwithstanding that it was last of the five different interoceanic railways to be built, it is already very popular and a big competitor of the American lines. The company tries as hard as possible; it has excellent cars and provides an opportunity for good dining; the staff is very polite and the fares are not higher than the other Pacific railways. Because of its steamboats on the big lakes and because of a number of branch lines up to the American border, the connections with other railways are outstanding. Since it is the only railway that cuts North America from east to west without the aid of others, it also operates the longest one-piece track, namely from Montreal to Vancouver, which takes 6 days and 6 nights.

From Vancouver, at the Pacific Ocean, the company has recently been running its own steamship line to Asia for which the English government has pledged a yearly subsidy of 45,000 pounds sterling and the Canadian government an amount of 15,000 pounds sterling. For those amounts, it maintains three beautiful steamships of 6,000 tons, which compete with both American lines based in San Francisco, and in that way she maintains the shortest route between Europe and Japan. It is, therefore, easier for the English to make a journey around the world; from now on, one can purchase a ticket for 675 dollars in London or Liverpool.

The Canadian Pacific maintains various types of rail cars and is therefore very suitable for colonists who settle in these areas. Besides the common but very tidy Pullman-sleepers, one also finds tourist-sleepers which are much more plainly decorated, but for a dollar a night still provides a good bed; in one of them, I saw a kitchen with a fired stove where the travelling families could prepare what they wanted. Furthermore, one can spend the night in free colonist-cars on pullout benches; this is free of charge, but one is expected to look after their own blankets.

Further, at the loveliest parts an observation car is coupled on, to which everyone has access without paying extra. Just as in the regular cars, one meets a nice combination of various professions and social classes, which makes it more attractive because the public in these areas is polite and of a good sort. Of course, amongst them there is no shortage of some representatives of the servants of the High Church, "men of the world" from head to toe, who seem to consider as their principal activity travelling in the highest comfort and, in gratitude, hold now and then a short sermon or read a few prayers in the best and largest hotels.

One normally dines at certain stations for 75 cents per meal. With everything one notices not being in the USA anymore, because there is not that same rushing, one is allowed a half-hour to eat at one's ease and one is warned by an announcer about the departure of the train. In the absence of a good dining station, sometimes a dinner-car is coupled, which is very neatly decorated and where a complete meal is served for the same price.

I do not want to describe all the panoramas that one gets to see along the whole line, a distance so large that the time has to be reset three times. I want to restrict myself to the loveliest, most western part, which is in no way inferior to even the Denver and Rio Grande R. R. in Colorado. In the observation car, open on all sides, where one can enjoy the view undisturbed, the lovely scenes continuously captivate the public who are quite prepared to be exposed to smoke, soot and dust. I do not know a more beautiful railway in the world and shall therefore try to give a fair description of it. Only a few brief annotations made while travelling make up the following account.

As I have said before, the line starts at the west coast in Vancouver. The next year (1892), the railway which connects this city with Tacoma shall be completed. But, for the time being, one travels down there by steamer through the Puget Sound via Victoria. The many vessels that sail through the large bay are roomy, well-equipped and supplied with excellent meals. The coasts along which we sail do resemble the Swedish landscape; they are not grand but very lovely and picturesque especially the young prosperous cities. With their wooden houses and surrounded by green forests, they expand against the hills at the edges of the smooth water surface.

Victoria, the capital of British Columbia is beautifully located at the southern tip of the large Vancouver Island. The splendid entrance into the spacious harbour during a calm sea gives a picture of peace and rest, and does resemble the Norwegian fjords. When one walks through the city, it is pretty; although her total outlook is truly American. Still, one notices all kinds of little things as if one has arrived in an English city. One can see it in the character of the stores, the architectural style of the houses, the clothing of the men and women, and the politeness of the residents.

One arrives in Vancouver the next morning. It has already developed into an important city, especially after the big fire of 1886 that left all houses in ash, sharing the fate with which all large cities in this corner of America seem to be hit. Tacoma, Seattle and Spokane in the last ten years were all almost completely destroyed by fire, but each rose with rejuvenated power out of her ruins.

The first part of the railway runs along the Fraser River. At the beginning, this is a peaceful stream with flat banks but half a day travelling by train takes us miles away through the grand Fraser Canyon, where the river meanders between the steep cliffs hundreds of feet below us.

A few hours later, completely different scenery awaits us. We ride closely along a number of dark green lakes, not very different from those in Scotland. But this beautiful spot must also make room for another place. We arrive in an area full of rugged, endless forests, where everything lays jumbled up and here and there appear a few Indian huts. A mass of trunks and stumps are carried away with the mountain stream and it is a wild romantic view to see them mixed up, half weather-stained in the lakes. At many places the forest is on fire and there are a number of half-charred trunks standing smoldering and smoking. Once or twice it had happened that the rails expanded through the heat and buckled, making the trains derail and end up among the burning wood.

Near Revelstoke, we pass the Columbia River that almost twelve hours later shall cut our path for the second time. To the north, this wonderful stream makes a large bend that is cut by a section of the railway. This part belongs to the loveliest of places. After we have gone through the Albert Canyon, where the train stops five minutes in the middle of the track to give the passengers the opportunity to cast a view to the abyss from a protruding rock point, we cut straight through the Selkirk mountain range. To climb to the upper-reaches of the Illecilleweat River, the track makes an enormous loop and later we climb high above the Bear Creek and other valleys, through a number of snow-sheds and over a number of viaducts. The viaduct in the Beaver Canyon is like the one near Amsteg at the Gotthardbahn, supported by upright pillars, and is 450 feet long and 300 feet high making the highest railway bridge that was ever built from wood. By that way, we slowly arrive into the midst of the snow-covered rocks and, for the moment, reach our highest point in the Rogers Pass (4,275 ft.), which was named after Major A. B. Rogers who discovered it in 1883.

For the second time, we descended into the valley of the Columbia, which we cross at Donald where the clock is advanced one hour. Again, it is necessary for the train to climb up the other side through the Wapta Canyon and is now even higher than before.

At the Stephen station, the railway reaches its summit at 5,296 feet (1615 metres) in the Kicking Horse Pass. This peculiar name (kicking) is probably coincidentally derived from the obstreperous

CPR bridge across Columbia River at Revelstoke, 1888-1892

CPR Locomotive 313 on Kicking Horse Bridge, Alberta

behavior of the horse of one of the surveyors, who measured the terrain for the railway construction. Better chosen is the name of the more than 12,000-foot-high Mount Stephen, at the foot of which the pass is located, and which was named after the president of the Canadian Pacific.

A few hours later, we arrive in Banff where the company has built a large hotel. From the high-situated building, one has a beautiful view of the valley of the Bow River, which flows to the east into the Saskatchewan, which runs to Lake Winnipeg that empties her waters into Hudson's Bay. The surroundings of Banff are abundant with therapeutic hot sulphur springs and shall probably in due time become a frequented health resort for rheumatics and sufferers of other ailments. Moreover, the government, in following the Yellowstone Park, has now set apart a large area of 100,000 acres as a National Park. Here, however, hunting with guns is yet not forbidden, so that hunters can still shoot to their heart's content at wild cats, pumas, bears, deer and mountain sheep. However, there is already talk about protecting the not-dangerous animals living in the wild against the hunt and also limiting fishing, which the Englishmen are so keen about. I was more pleased by the simpler, but much cozier Glacier House, a half-day by rail located more to the west on the railway. It is located at the foot of the mountain, Sir Donald (11,000 feet), named after the railway director Sir Donald Smith. The top has not been climbed as yet, and it is said that a prize of 1,000 dollars and a free ticket for the Canadian Pacific is offered as a reward for the first conquest. This seems to be rather unlikely, because the climb seems to me, on the whole, not so exceptionally problematic and if I had had my alpine equipment with me, I would have gladly tested my powers on it.

I cannot urge anyone enough, who might visit this remote area of the earth, in Heaven's name, not to hurry through, but to stop for one day in Glacier House. One would think that the large Illecillewaet Glacier, which comes down from Mount Donald, can be satisfactorily

Glacier House, British Columbia, 1887-1889

admired from the railway; this is however a mistake. The glacier can easily withstand comparison to the most beautiful in Switzerland and when we approach it, it looks completely different again than when it is seen from a distance. As it is with all truly majestic scenes of nature, they cannot be captured with a single glance, for that they consider themselves too sublime. They need just the same as a work of art needs, to be studied in order to firstly show their many-sided beautiful angles and then we should take the time to let the grandeur dawn upon us and adapt our consciousness to the unusual dimension which surrounds us. But, we also discover at every turn new beautiful angles which, at first, still escape from our view.

The walk to the foot of the glacier was through a field of roughly mixed up boulders, along smashed bridges and immensely large chopped-down trunks that proved not to be resistant against the fiercely rushing stream — everything was dragged along the mountain stream in its course. This is not the only thing that one associates with Glacier House and it is worth it to get off at this station.

On a quiet September morning, I walked up to Marion Lake, which is concealed high in the mountains among the woods. The steep footpath appeared to be hardly trod upon, because of a number of cobwebs strung across the path and, a large prairie chicken which I came across was so tame that I could almost grab it. The footpath meandered through a true primal forest, occasionally over crushed and crumbled rocks, then again over a carpet of moss, moldered wood and tree bark among the wonderful pine trees draped with light green hairy moss. Finally, we got to the top. It is deathly quiet — no bird is heard, no fish splashes in the water, only a few water nymphs buzz on the shore. The slender, transparent, motionless pine trees are reflected in the fine, rippling, dark green water, where branches and tree trunks lay to molder on the shallow bottom. The snow-crowned rocks rise above the forest, along its sides glaciers hang down and on one side of the little lake, a large avalanche of rock boulders has made a path to the water surface and swept the trees along on its way down. It is a scene never to forget and, deeply touched, we returned homewards fulfilled with the great enjoyment that the Canadian Pacific Railway provided us."

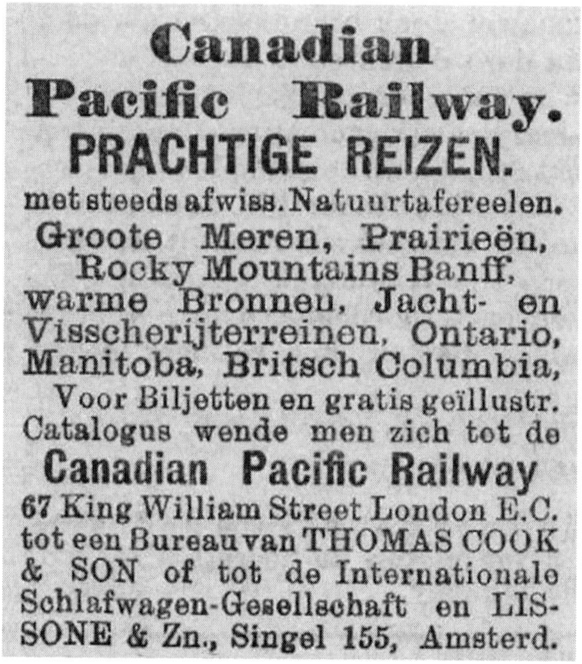

Advertisement in *Het Nieuws van den Dag*, April 22, 1899

Chapter Fifteen
To the Canadian Arctic, 1875

Laurens R. Koolemans Beijnen

Laurens R. Koolemans Beijnen

During the 1850s and 1860s, the Netherlands suffered a period of malaise and apathy, lacking an enterprising desire. This was called *Jan Salie Geest* in the Netherlands, Jan Salie being the patron of all sleepyheads.[125] Only when this influence dissipated would the country finally revert to the spirit of the 17th century, an economic power surveying the seas around the world, regaining its worthy position amongst the world powers.[126]

News of the prevailing dark mood in Holland also reached the Dutch East Indies and had its effect on a young navy lieutenant, Laurens Reinhard Koolemans Beijnen. During his period of service, he noted that the Royal Dutch Navy had lost much of its seamanship and seaman's spirit. Being a dedicated naval officer and having obvious nationalistic leanings he wished to lift the country's mood with a captivating venture. An Arctic expedition seemed to be an excellent way to revive not only the seamen's spirit in the navy and merchant fleet, but also the national spirit.

Upon his return from the Indies and with this idea in mind he approached Naval Councillor, Captain M. H. Jansen. Through his contacts, Jansen was able to arrange a place for Koolemans Beijnen on the British polar expedition of 1875 so he could study the navigation of the western Arctic waters. An additional motive to team up with the expedition was to gain further experience in the Arctic so as to lay groundwork for the initiation of an exclusively Dutch expedition to the Arctic. The 1875 summer expedition to the Arctic was made aboard the *Pandora*, which sailed under the command of the famous English polar explorer, Sir Allen Young.[127]

After returning home, Koolemans Beijnen wrote a report about his journey for the Minister of the Navy, which was published the following year by the *Aardrijkskundig Genootschap* ('Geographic Society'). This extract from that publication is about the part of the journey that took place in Canadian territory and the exciting discovery made by the author.

The *Pandora* left England and crossed the Northern Atlantic, sailing into Davis Strait on July 28. It would navigate further northwards along the Greenland coast to the point where it would enter Canadian territory.

Route of the expedition of the Pandora, 1875 (Source T. Bal)

"While steaming forward with a cold northern wind on August 18, 1875, at six o'clock in the evening, we reached the most northwestern point of Carey Island. Although there was almost a storm blowing, we still went on shore to deliver messages.

The Carey Islands, discovered in 1618 by Baffin,[128] *are located on the route to Smith Sound. They are uninhabited and look very rugged and desolate. Various small glaciers reach out into the sea. The highest point of the most northwestern part of the island is 292 metres high. There was great disappointment when three old cairns were found, since there was absolutely no evidence that Captain Nares had been here. One of the cairns, erected in July 1867, by whalers from Dundee, had contained a message saying that from the highest point here, absolutely no ice was to be seen. The cairn also contained half a bottle of rum and a piece of chewing tobacco for the honest finder. Another cairn located on the other end of the island had already been opened earlier. It contained almost nothing. The only thing we found was an old, very rusted can, burst open. Painted on it were difficult to distinguish white letters reading "Resolut & Assista", from which one could infer that this cairn was erected by the English Government vessels* Resolute *and* Assistance.[129]

Captain Young assumed that the government vessels were prevented, through mist or storm, from calling at this island group, and therefore a cairn was erected on the spot, where we left behind messages in two drums. Not without difficulty, we returned on board

*in the light of a midnight sun because the wind had much increased
and there was a high sea.*

*Straightaway the sail was set and, coursing to the SW, we entered
Lancaster Sound[130] on the morning of August 21. The previous day,
at the height of Cape Horsburgh, two polar bears were killed and one
was caught alive. According to English seamen, it is safest to keep to
the north side of Lancaster Sound, since there are a number of safe
ports. Captain Parker of the Truelove, an old and enterprising whaler,
gives the following advice: "When one wants to enter Lancaster
Sound and one is overtaken by severe weather from the NW, then keep
right away for the northern shore, to use the northern wind that will
blow there and avoid the lower shore. During a storm from the west,
keep likewise along the north shore of the Sound and be aware that the
stream runs along the southern shore to the east".*

*The Pandora[131] now kept to the northern shore and although
she had to sail straightaway through a lot of drift ice that was much
heavier than we had seen in Melville Bay, she held her course very
well. The coast of North Devon posed at starboard like an ice wall,
where now and then the peaks towered above.*

*At this time of the year, Lancaster Sound is always found to be
open, so Captain Young was very surprised when near the evening of
August 22, the ice became thicker and thicker and by ten o'clock the
Pandora was stopped in her course by an ice dam in the middle of a
thick fog. During the night it was impossible to see anything through
the fog, so the Pandora was forced to keep a slow southeasterly course.*

*When, near four o'clock in the morning the scud lifted, we clearly
saw the southern shore straight in front of us but an endless ice mass
also blocked the passage here. Keeping the horizon to the south leading
to the east, we saw on a vast flat of about 8 p. [compass points], that
is a sharp clear white stripe above the horizon known as 'ice sky',
which signals the presence of large ice masses. Above the stripe are
cumulus clouds, with a dark veil of clouds on both sides because it
usually reveals the presence of water. The hope was born to be able
to push through the ice at one or two places. We had just seen that
going southwards was impossible, so then we followed for the next 8 p.
the unpromising ice clouds, and then later the dark clouds. However,
that was just in the direction from which the Pandora had come.*

Nevertheless, from the crow's nest it seemed that the waterway was in fact open, and it was quite possible that an opening in the ice was overlooked during the thick fog, while a stiff breeze from the ENE would perhaps disperse the ice wall from the northern shore.

Therefore, the course taken was once again to the northern shore. At one o'clock, we were at the fringe of the solid ice. So far as I could see from the crow's nest with my binoculars, I saw nothing other than a solid, dense white snow covering a hilly ice mass that nowhere promised passage. Here and there was only a small ice-hole, however this soon dissolved in the compact ice-mass.

Until the morning of August 23, we tried in vain to figure out whether it was the wind or the tide that caused the motion in the ice.

Finally, close to noon, near the southern shore, we saw lots of water, aided by a stiff SE wind that pushed the ice from shore. We also encountered a strong stream to the east, which broke off the ice field along the southern shore, transporting it along. The Pandora managed to advance against the southern shore from one open ice-hole to the other, finally reaching open water.

As soon as possible, we sailed to the west, keeping the high coast located on larboard and the endless ice field on starboard. From the crow's nest, Admiralty Inlet seemed frozen over, yet we hurried by it to get into more open water because the barometer dropped quickly, and severe blizzards, alternated by thick fog, did of course increase the danger of the immediate proximity of land. In one thick fog, at about six o'clock in the evening, there was a close call as the Pandora would have had steered, at a speed of five miles, into a huge iceberg in the centre of the waterway, which floated toward us with a brisk SW wind. Easing up the sails and laying the helm to starboard was just enough to evade this great danger, however not without making a hard jolt against a part of it which was protruding underwater, suddenly stopping the Pandora's track. At first, everybody thought that we had become stranded on a submerged rock, yet we were soon reassured when it turned out that the ship had suffered no further damage.

Meanwhile, the wind from the SE increasingly continued to chill, and the barometer was dropping, which made our situation no less dangerous. The next day it was foggy with bitter weather, all the while a fine wet snow fell ceaselessly. As a thick fog continuously hovered over the ship, neither land nor water was to be seen at some distance, while in the vicinity of the Pandora large ice fields repeatedly turned up. The compasses were absolutely unusable and the sun was invisible, so that one had to steer the ship by the pennant in the crow's nest, of course then always trusting that the wind would keep blowing from the same direction.

Since, it was impossible to know with enough certainty where we were positioned, one sail was taken down. At eleven o'clock in the morning, the fog lifted a little and suddenly a steep, high table land became visible in the NW, right in front of the larboard bow. Broaching to the wind and tacking was only a moment's work, so that the Pandora was positioned in SE direction. The coastline was a very high plateau and because the coast is almost all tabular shaped, it gave no opportunity to explore it. Since Captain Young thought that it had to be the coast of North Devon Island, near noon we sailed southward and shortly thereafter in a southwesterly direction.

High rocks on both coasts, unknown streams, an unusable compass, no sun, no leads on the map to spy out, and then the whole day a thick fog, accompanied with wet fine snow, made sailing Barrow Strait[132] daunting.

The next day, the state of the weather was not much better and only under small sail the vessel steered westwards. At six o'clock in the evening, however, the cold and dry wind blew from the north, pushed the fog quickly forwards, making the coast show up only one mile from us on starboard. It turned out that the Pandora had arrived at the height of Cape Griffith and was thus not far from Beechy Island. Soon we also saw the island on the horizon, although we anchored there not 'til midnight, because the Pandora had to steam against a stiff northern wind.

The main reason why we called at Beechy Island was that Captain Young had decided to replenish the provisions of his vessel from the supplies, which were left behind here in 1854 by the North Star's Captain Saunders, with the purpose of furnishing this island as a refuge for the crews of English exploration ships, in case one or more would have been destroyed by the ice.

Eighteen years ago when Captain Young, as lieutenant on board the Fox, had called on Beechy Island, everything was still in good condition and after that time no ship had gone farther. Although the wind blew stiffly, Captain Young went straightaway on shore to see the condition of the provisions with his own eyes. The wooden shed, known by the name Northumberland House, had been forcibly opened and our first impression was that everything had been dragged out and smashed up. The intruders had forced their way through the windows at the south side of the hut and at various places had ripped off planks. Bundles of beautiful blue cloth and warm woolen blankets, just like bundles of fine flannel were also hauled out of the hut and were partially shredded. All kinds of garments, including hundreds of pairs of socks and mittens, laid scattered all over in the greatest disorder. Numerous drums filled with all kinds of stuff were stacked up outside the hut and scattered on all sides. A few skeletons of seals made it instantly clear to us that polar bears had been the pillagers here.

Furthermore, a number of sleds were scattered around the house, as well as an old crow's nest, a pile of coal, a cooking stove and other Arctic requisites. On the beach laid the small yacht, Mary, brought here by Ross,[133] as well as two large old lifeboats, still in rather good condition. Going inside through the broken door, we saw however that most of the provisions had been saved. Through the openings in the hut, a lot of snow and rain had certainly blown in and this had thawed, and then froze again, creating a crust of ice that had increased every year in size, hermetically sealing almost the complete stock from the outside world. The provisions were (not without difficulty) taken out from under the ice and brought on board with sloops. So also were numerous cans of pemmican, barrels with flour, sugar, chocolate and many other articles taken on board the Pandora. This task was finished at six o'clock.

The gravesite of the respected French marine officer Bellot[134] had been damaged a bit by the weather, however, the marble tombstone of Franklin[135] was still as good as new and it was easy to read the following inscription:

To the memory of Franklin, Crozier, Fitsjames and all their gallant brother officers and faithful companions who have suffered and perished in the cause of science and the service of their country, this tablet is erected, near the spot where they passed their first Arctic winter and whence they issued forth to conquer difficulties or to die.

It commemorates the grief of their admiring countrymen and friends, and the anguish, subdued by faith of her, who has lost, in the heroic leader of the expedition, the most devoted and affectionate of husbands.

And so HE bringeth them into the haven, where they would be.

At eight o'clock in the evening the anchor was lifted and a favourable wind pushed the ship quickly forward in the direction of Peel Sound. And now the pivotal part of our journey would come.

Earlier English explorers had found Peel Sound always closed off by ice and now the question was, whether Captain Young would be equally unlucky. There was every indication of it because the entire next day the course of the *Pandora* was continuously held up by vast ice fields, through which she steamed with great difficulties. Yet the ship made headway all the same and Limestone Island already became visible when the ship arrived at the boundary of the ice wall that blocked off the whole entrance of the strait. The rigging was heavily rimed which made it difficult to handle the yard and sails. Until the next morning, it remained dead calm, so that there was not the slightest movement in the vast ice fields on hills standing three to five metres high.

At 10 o'clock, the wind blew forcefully from the north, and to our surprise and pleasure, in a half-hour, an opening broke in the middle of the ice mass, through which the *Pandora* immediately moved closer to Limestone Island, while the opening behind her closed just as quickly because the wind turned to the east. Captain Young went ashore at Limestone Island, which I estimated to be 156 metres high, in order to get a better and farther view across the ice, and also to see whether there were remains to be found from a stock of foodstuffs that were left behind there by one of the officers of Sir Edward Belcher.[136] Fog, however, prevented Captain Young from seeing anything and the foodstuffs were not found. Before our departure, a message of our presence was left behind in a cairn. While we went searching around the island, we discovered the remains of old Eskimo settlements, *noticeable because of a circle of stones used by them to secure their hide tents.*

Captain Young believed, judging from the shape, that they dated back centuries. If we want to estimate approximately when the Eskimos had put up their tents at this lonely place, then we have to look for the answer to that question in the history of their old trails. Namely, at the time the Norsemen first discovered Greenland in the 11th century, they found an uninhabited, desolate land. During nearly two centuries of exceptional prosperity, they remained there. Afterward, they appeared to have been completely wiped out by a tribe, which they called Skraelings or Dwarfs, from which the present-day Eskimo descended.

A few observations gave the answer to the question: Where did the tribe come from? It is difficult to assume that they would have crossed over from Lapland to Greenland, because there they would have certainly left traces behind at Spitsbergen, Iceland or Jan Mayen Island. They have absolutely not the least similarity with the redskins of America, yet one quick glance is enough to see a strong likeness between them and the Mongolian race. Their dark skin, their raven hair, their jet black eyes which, just as with the Chinese, positioned a little slanted in the head, are reason enough to convince us that they originally belonged in Asia, the cradle of so many tribes. Besides, all along the coast of Parry Island, old remnants of Eskimo settlements are found, while precisely the same period that preceded the invasion by the Skraelings in Greenland, is also the time that Ghengis Khan, in Middle Asia, sent his wild hordes flooding like a torrent westwards and northwards over Tatarstan and Siberia. Thus, it could be possible that those conquerors had pushed aside the tribes along the northwest coast of Siberia and drove them in front of themselves. During the following weeks, they wandered to the Parry Islands[137] and, finding them uninhabited, they continued, driven by destitution farther and farther, until they finally arrived in Greenland. There, they found a completely different land where they could live. Having come across only a small colony of Norsemen, which they wiped out, they expanded, undisturbed, over the whole of Greenland.

So, it could also be possible that these restless ramblers from the high North, on their difficult trip across the frozen tundra of Siberia to the much more favoured hunting grounds of West Greenland, perhaps centuries ago, had pitched their tents at this barren place. They were probably expecting protection from the cutting northern wind at the bottom of the steep cliffs that encompassed the western point of Limestone Island.

As soon as Captain Young had returned on board, the ship steamed further southwards between Limestone Island and the mainland, yet she was again soon shrouded in a thick fog for the whole night. We now experienced the same difficulties with which we had become familiar in Barrow Strait, with one difference — any ship, so far as one knew, had never explored the rugged coast at larboard. The endless ice masses, as soon the wind changed, would push the vessel against the shore, so that in addition one was now forced to sail southwards as quickly as possible, to get out of this dangerous situation.

The whole night, the Pandora could do nothing other than as a blind man going by touch, led only by the wind that could shift at any moment and throw her on shore. Now and then, a sinister glimpse of the terrifying ice-mass to starboard constantly reminded her of her dangerous situation. The night passed without incident, however the next morning, we had the ice behind us and sailed southwards in completely open water.

H.M.S. *Pandora*

Now we were truly in Peel Sound. The Pandora *cut through water never before sailed by any other vessel, other than, perhaps, by the unlucky vessels* Erebus *and* Terror,[138] *whose brave crews, possibly in the same hopeful, happy mood as we are at present, were heading for their disaster. At noon, we passed a 'rookery of gulls' — there were thousands of these birds nesting in safety in this lonely remote place. The coast we followed was charted during a sledge journey by Sir James Ross.[139] The same evening, we arrived at the height of Cape Coulman and discovered there, well over twenty metres above the high water line, a cairn which contained a written message from Sir James Ross, dated June 7, 1849. This was replaced with a copy, whereby Captain Young enclosed his report and returned on board.*

The tide was found to be rising, running fast to the north, with the needle on the inclinometer showing $18\frac{1}{2}°$. For a while we used a different method to measure the vessel's position, because the compasses were completely unusable here. One calculated the correct course by measuring with the sextant the arch between an object straight ahead and the sun, whose real position was found in Sun's True Bearing Tables from Latitude 70° N–89° N. Prepared for the Arctic Expedition of 1875, *Hydrographic Office Admiralty, of which Captain Young retained a few examples. In these charts, the true bearing of the sun was shown for every hour of the day.*

In order not to run during the dark and foggy night in the channel of the islands, we slowly navigated back into the wind, this being the best way to keep the same course. In the early morning of August 30, the vessel set course further southwards. Everyone hoped that Bellot Strait would still be passed the same day. Our conviction was strengthened since we saw no ice, we had a favourable wind and, moreover, the weather was very mild, as if we had arrived in a completely new climate zone. However, we would soon see how wrong we were about this. The northern wind that prevailed during almost the whole winter had pushed a lot of ice from the polar region southward (which probably had opened up Smith Sound for the English government ships). For us, these winds had been less favourable, because they had pushed the ice out of Wellington Channel. For that reason, the floating ice masses had jammed the south of Peel Sound. At four o'clock, the Pandora *anchored in front of an endless ice mass, which closed off the whole strait. We were close alongside De La Roquette Islands. Fitz Roy Inlet was clearly visible and Cape Bird, where Bellot Strait ends, was only two geographical miles south of us.*

On August 25, it remained foggy until five o'clock in the afternoon, then it cleared up again and it turned out that the vessel had drifted near the immediate vicinity of the De La Roquette Islands. Captain Young went on in order to leave a message behind in a cairn and to be in a position to see farther out over the ice. From the top of the island we could clearly see how, in a southeasterly direction, the coast of Somerset with the high steep Cape 'Bird' which, under the name of Boothia Felix,[140] disappears from our sight in the far south. In the southwest, we noticed a high mountain ridge on the horizon being the SE point of Prince of Wales Island and, precisely between the two coasts in the direction of King William's Island, there was nothing else to see other than endless hills covered with ice. The prospect was bleak to the highest degree. With the exception of a few ice-holes, there was no open water to see. It was a dense mass, marbled with a lot of old ice. If it was possible to penetrate up to Bellot Strait, then much would be gained, because one could turn in there, anchor the vessel somewhere safe, and wait for the moment when the ice drifted perhaps a little more northward past the strait, making it possible to push out farther southwards.

The next day no favourable changes occurred in the condition of the ice. The ship, anchored in a bay that was as if it were formed by ice, was carried along in a solid ice mass that was being pushed northward by a southerly wind. An iceberg that we had seen ten miles south of us the previous day had now drifted closely to the ship. The rising tide, it was learned, ran to the north, and new ice quickly started to form during the day. The question was whether the Pandora would become ice-bound and winter here, or whether she would try to get out of Peel Sound again. Yet, if she wanted the latter, then this had to happen quickly.

It was now already September 3. On August 30, there had been a new moon and even the spring tide did not have the might to break the ice wall. It was clear to everyone that there was no hope of pushing on to King William Island this year. Besides, by over-wintering here, nothing would be gained. The coast was mapped by Captain Young in 1859 during a sledge journey, and if King William Island would be reached in the spring, then one would still find nothing more than Captain M'Clintock[141] did, because, just as then, the ground would be covered with snow.

Besides, there were not sufficient provisions on board to wait until August to determine then whether the ship would be freed from the ice. So one should try to reach Beechy Island in the spring in order to get farther from there in the sloops and so that the thus-far accident-free journey would not end in catastrophe. To winter in Peel Sound would be nothing other then a pointless waste of energy and materials.

On September 3, when the vessel was in imminent danger of becoming trapped in again, thanks to the ice that came drifting from the north in large quantities, Captain Young decided to retreat. He, as all of us, was profoundly disappointed. There had been beautiful evenings when we watched the sun set, when she shrouded the peaks of the snow-covered mountains in a beautiful scarlet cloth and, from behind the entire mountain ridge, her last rays cast dancing shadows on the endless ice field of De La Roquette Islands. Not one ripple was evident on the dark glassy surface of the Sound. The water, by its own making, being handcuffed, buffeted under the self-imposed burden, laid weary, quiet in its ice cold clasp and where the sun, in soft purple splendour, radiates the thousands of ridges of the motionless ice mass. One imagined oneself to stand on the fringe of an immense cemetery, above which the white marble grave-pillars lost themselves in a colourful medley in the wide vista, shrouded in that mysterious, incredible light of the solemn, calm, twilight hours of a polar world.

But now we were on our voyage home and soon it proved that it was high time for it. With a fully reduced mainsail, the Pandora sailed out of Peel Sound again and, on the evening of September 4, passed Limestone Island. We had barely passed it when we saw at larboard a vast ice field looming, which threatened to cut off the vessel's return journey. However, as Captain Young believed to see a small open waterway against the land ice between the snow drifts, he decided to try to make immediate use of it, and to reach Cape Grinnell[142] before the encroaching ice would enclose us due to a storm from the northwest pushing the ice rapidly to the coast. It was the only chance left to us, if we did not want to be locked up during the whole winter in Peel Sound. Because the darkness started to set in quickly, we steamed up as fast as possible.

It was a terrible night. The wind picked up to become a severe storm, accompanied with hail and blizzards, and the Pandora worked its way with great difficulty with on one side, the white glare from the enclosing ice, and the high snow-covered coast close to us on the other. Only a few times during this stormy night did a single star show in the sky, which gave the man on the helm a fixed point by which to navigate. While the wind was increasing, the thermometer dropped to 18° F and the foam of the waves transformed into a layer of ice as it splashed over the deck. At midnight, the snow lay a foot deep on the deck while the view became almost obscured by the whirling snow, which was driven out of the folds of the sails. In this way, the Pandora proceeded until three o'clock, when we suddenly saw an ice wall directly in front of us and, being so close, that only by making a sharp manoeuvre, were we able to sail just clear of it. Fortunately, the fog lifted a bit in time and convinced the commander that the Pandora had arrived in the immediate vicinity of Cape Grinnell, which, partially covered with snow in the dark of night, appeared ghostly.

For merely a moment, this apparition became visible in front of our eyes; the next moment, utter darkness prevailed again. In this way, the Pandora laid three anxious hours close to the wind. When the weather cleared again, from the crow's nest some movements were seen in the ice by which we could descry its weak points. Immediately, the vessel was steered in that direction and it succeeded (under several sails and steaming to capacity) to break through the weakest spot, and to reach the open waterway of Barrow Strait. Under a tightly reefed main sail, the Pandora dashed on, now pushed by stormy weather from the WNW, through Barrow Strait and Lancaster Sound, without seeing any more ice, although we still had to really keep a lookout during the dark night. In such weather, it is incredibly difficult to distinguish a protruding ice mass a little above the waterline from the white curly crests of the waves. A collision with an ice formation underneath the water could have disastrous consequences for the vessel and crew.

On September 7, the Pandora was again in open north water and Captain Young decided to attempt, yet one more time, to find a trace of the government vessels, by exploring Carey Island once more again.

If he would find nothing there, he would attempt to move along to Littleton Island, hoping to return to England by that way with some record of the expedition. So far, never had earlier expedition vessels sailed at this latitude that late in the year. Before September 5, they had already all moved into their winter quarters. The necessity for doing so was soon shown by the ship. Beforehand, our commander had taken the precaution to reef all sails tight, and this was a good thing because they were now unmanageable. Rigging and poles were completely covered with ice and the hull of the vessel was one lump of ice. The seawater, when it swept over, fell as ice on the deck. One could walk only with great difficulty over the rocking and slippery deck. The sails had become as stiff as planks, so that, for example, the lowering of the jib was an unsolvable problem. In addition, heavy weather from the NNW accompanied a heavy snowstorm and a high, choppy, difficult sea.

On the 10th, the Pandora *was situated at the most southeast of the Carey Islands, on the highest point of which a cairn was discovered. The island now had a completely different appearance. Instead of showing nothing other than bare stones, it was covered under an uninterrupted white blanket of snow. In order to investigate the cairn, the* Pandora *heaved to and the Lieutenants Lillingston and Koolemans Beijnen went ashore. The highest point of the island, which was 170 metres high, was only reached through a great deal of effort since one repeatedly sank into the snow crust up to the hips, from time to time sliding quite a bit backward. The cold northern wind that howled over the peak caused clothing to freeze into a firm snow clump necessitating a fast return, however not without having first removed from the cairn a small tin canister. Upon examination once back on board, it proved to hold a sealed package addressed to the Admiralty. At last, a message had been discovered of H. M. Alert and H. M. Discovery!*

Since the commander deemed that it was not advisable to steer further northwesterly in this weather, the bow was turned and the Pandora *sailed with her mainsails furled before the wind toward the south. During the night of September 12, she passed the last drifting ice at the latitude of Cape York finally arriving at 2 o'clock a.m. on September 19 by Lievely Harbour, Disco Island [Greenland].*

Final Words

"Should the willing reader share a small bit of the same joy that I had, not only during the journey, but even the joy that I experienced by writing my journal, then I consider the time spent on writing it not completely lost and I consider my work fully rewarded."

Bernard Schuijlenburg shared these thoughts in the preface to his book, *Amerika en Canada, Reisaantekeningen*. Not only can we relate to these comments but we would also suggest that he, in a sense, speaks for all of the travellers who had the patience and fortitude to put their travel experiences about Canada on paper. The time spent doing so is not lost and therefore, can be "considered" fully rewarded.

We are greatly indebted to these 'Dutch Gentlemen' who chose to visit even a small part of this vast, and to most of their countrymen, unknown land. We could not help but appreciate their collective perceptiveness and their individual diligence in recording their views and impressions. It has been said that travel journals have their shortcomings — they often reveal so much of the personal and cultural biases of the writer in ways that scholarly writing should not. Nevertheless, their extensive education and worldly sophistication were behind the unexpected depth of their diverse opinions, thereby creating unique insights into many aspects of 19th century Canada and her intriguing history.

Schuijlenburg also wrote:

"I am aware of the small value of my writing and pretty well know that my journal, in book form presented to the public at large, will soon take a forgotten place between the unread works of the careless, who bought it on a whim. Or even worse, that it will never leave the publisher's warehouse or stock rooms of some booksellers."

It was fascinating to trace these journals and letters, and rewarding to connect the stories of adventure and discovery into a single volume. Schuijlenburg and the other gentlemen would be gratified to know that their travel experiences were not lost or forgotten — that both the actual and the virtual booksellers of the 21st century will deliver these stories, to be enjoyed again by a wider audience, more than 100 years after they were first published.

Appendix A
Traveller Biographies

Karel D. W. Boissevain

The text is from: Karel D. W. Boissevain, "Brieven uit Canada", printed in *Algemeen Handelsblad*, April 14, April 26 and May 15 (Amsterdam 1892).

Boissevain, born in Amsterdam in 1866, was a member of a wealthy and influential Dutch family. The firm owned by his uncle, Adolphe Boissevain, was a major investor of the CPR during its construction. Upon his doctor's advice, Karel Boissevain, a former navy officer, came to Canada as a therapy for his asthma in 1891. After working for a number of months as a surveyor for the CPR, in 1892, he travelled on the CPR from the Crowsnest Pass to Montreal. That same year, he married his sweetheart from Holland, Wilhelmina de Vos. Boissevain and his family lived in Montreal for a number of years. In 1895, he was appointed as the Dutch Consul-General. He held this post until 1902, after which he returned with his family to Holland. Boissevain passed away at Geneva, Switzerland in 1944.

Frederik Christiaan Colenbrander

The text is from: Personal letters sent to his family from Canada in 1893, Regionaal Archief Zutphen, Nr. 210, Familie Colenbrander en de erven van Sytzama 1720–1985, Inv. Nr. 130 Brieven ingekomen van reis door USA en Canada.

Frederik Christiaan Colenbrander was born on June 14, 1868 in Brummen, Netherlands. He was the owner of the brick factory, *De Konijnenwaard*, in Brummen, and various large land holdings. He lived throughout his life at the family country house, Reuversweerd, near Brummen. Colenbrander served as Dike Grave of the Polder District Brummensche Bandijk and also held the title of Lord of Millingen. In 1896, he obtained his Doctorate of Laws at the University of Utrecht. It is possible that during his trip he purchased some land in Illinois, since archival evidence regarding his estate mentions Illinois land holdings.

His mother was Jacoba Mispelblom Bijer and, through her side of the family, Colenbrander was related to one of his travel companions, Conrad van de Merwede Quarles van Ufford. Quarles van Ufford, a Notary, was born in Haarlem in 1863, of the sons of Philip Everhard Jonkheer Quarles van Ufford and Johanna Gerharda Mispelblom Beijer. Colenbrander's uncle Henricus 'Henk' Leembruggen was married to Henrietta Jacoba Dorothea Maria Mispelblom Bijer, and is mentioned by Colenbrander as a supporter of the first Dutch emigration to Winnipeg in 1893.

Through a series of marriages, the prominent family of his mother had become very well-connected in Dutch society. Her family began its business ventures in Zutphen as wine merchants in 1748. In 1770, they started a brandy distillery, which continued successfully for two centuries. Later on, family members were also involved in banking and accumulated vast holdings of real estate through which they yielded considerable influence. Colenbrander passed away on November 20, 1914 in Brummen and, with his death, the Colenbrander line to which he belonged became extinct in 1933.

Claude August Crommelin

The text used is from: *Een Amsterdammer in Amerika 1866–1867, Verslag van de reis van Claude August in door de Verenigde Staten en Canada*, Guus Veenendaal and H. Roger Grant, ed., Amsterdam: De Bataafsche Leeuw, 2009, pages 69–70 (published from a photocopy of the original travel journal).

Crommelin was born on March 1, 1840 in Amsterdam into a prominent family of businessmen. He received his primary education from a Swiss Governor and a private boarding school. In 1865, he received his Doctorate in Law from the University of Utrecht. After his American journey, Crommelin started a law office in Amsterdam and was later elected as a member of the Amsterdam City Council. Crommelin is also recognized as a pioneer in Dutch photography. On November 5, 1874, he took his own life by shooting himself through the head. He was 34 years old.

Johan C. Gevers

The text used is from a letter written by Johan C. Gevers to the then Minister of Foreign Affairs: "At sea on board of the ship *Le Havre*", dated August 5, 1845. Source letter: N.A. Tweede Afdeling, Ministerie van Buitenlandse zaken 1813–1870, Inv. Nr. 1381.

Baron Gevers was born in 1806 in Rotterdam into a family of the lower nobility, carrying the title of *Jonkheer*. In 1827, he started his career as a diplomat with the Department of Foreign Affairs in The Hague. In 1842, he was appointed Counselor of the Legation and Minister Plenipotentiary in the USA, a position he held until 1845. Before taking up his post in Stuttgart as residing Minister for Bayern, Wurtenberg and Baden, he decided to make a short trip to Canada. He set out his experiences in a letter to the Minister of Foreign Affairs, to whom he reported. Gevers returned to America in 1855 where he served as Dutch Envoy Extraordinary and Minister Plenipotentiary. That same year he married Catharina Mary Wright, daughter of US Senator William Wright, in Newark, New Jersey. In 1857, Gevers was authorized to carry the hereditary title of Baron. Gevers held a number of high diplomatic posts during the period between 1857 and 1871, retiring with an honourable dismissal. He passed away the year afterward, in Bonn, Germany.

Willem Theodore Gevers-Deynoot

The text is from: Willem T. Gevers-Deynoot, *Aantekeningen op eene reis door de Verenigde Staten van Noord-Amerika en Canada in 1859*, s'Gravenhage: Martinus Nijhof, 1860, pages 71–108.

Gever-Deynoot was born in 1808 in Wassenaar, Holland to a family of nobility, carrying the title of *Jonkheer*. He studied law at the University of Leiden where he obtained a doctorate (*magna cum laude*) in 1824. Afterward, he spent his career at the Dutch High Court. Amongst the many positions he held, he was a Member of the Dutch Lower House from 1852 to 1879, the year he died. He travelled to the USA and Canada in 1859 with a cousin Jonkheer C. T. W. Gevers. His reason for making this journey was "to inform the folks at home about 'important territories'."

Laurens Rijnhard Koolemans Beijnen

The text is from Laurens R. Koolemans Beijnen, *De Reis Der Pandora naar de Noordpoolgewesten in den zomer van 1875 door L. R. Koolemans Beijnen*, Amsterdam: C. F. Stemler, 1876, pages 50–65.

Lieutenant Koolemans Beijnen was born in 1852 in The Hague where his father was a pharmacist. At the age of twenty, he completed his education at the Royal Institute of the Navy in Den Helder. His first sea voyage was in 1872 to the Guinea Coast of Africa, aboard the *Wassenaar*. In 1874, he returned from Atjeh, Sumatra. He had always been interested in the 'North' and made this interest known to one of his superiors. Eventually, through the intervention of King Willem III of The Netherlands, and by having been granted time off from Willem Frederik van Erp Taalman Kip, the Minister of the Navy, he obtained a place on the British vessel, Pandora. She sailed in 1875 to the Canadian north. Koolemans Beijnen died by his own hand in 1879 while aboard the *H.M.S. Macasser*, serving in the Dutch East Indies.

Klaas Jacobs Kuipers

This text is from; *Een Groninger Zeeman In Napoleontische Tijd, Zee-en landreizen van Klaas J. Kuipers, Kleine Handelsvaart Contra Continental Stelsel*, J. Klatter, ed., Zutphen: De Walburg Pers, 1980, pages 87–89, republished from K. J. Kuipers' original book, published in 1844.

Kuipers was born August 9, 1778 to a middle-class family in Obergum. He spent his early years in Groningen, located in the northeastern part of the Netherlands. At an early age, he decided upon a career at sea and began working as a sailor at the age of twelve. Having first spent three years sailing on inland rivers and canals, he graduated to more choppy waters. In 1811, two weeks after a trip from Archangel, Russia to London, England, he signed on with the British vessel *Prospect*, chartered to pick up a load of pine masts in Quebec. After spending a number weeks in Quebec, during which he did some sightseeing, he left Canada on August 11, 1811 for Portsmouth, England. The next year, he concluded his career at sea and married Fenna Kornelis Zijlman, on April 28, 1819 in Winsum, as in the Netherlands.

Jan Rudolf Mees

The text used is from: Jan Rudolf Mees, *Dagboek Van eene Reis Door Amerika*. Rotterdam: Stichting Historische Publicaties Roterodamun, 1988, pages 17–19 and 55–63.

Mees was born in 1819 in Rotterdam, the son of Jacob Mees, the founder of an important trading house. Jan Mees went to the USA in 1843 aboard the *Britannia*, of the Cunard Steamship Company. His stated objective for the trip was to learn how to do business, particularly with respect to tobacco farming and trade in Virginia, USA in which his father's firm was involved. His excursion to Canada was probably more for pleasure than for business. Mees returned home in 1844, after which he began working at his father's firm. In 1847, he married Joanna Dunlop. Mees passed away in 1863 at the age of 44 in Baden-Baden, Germany, survived by his wife and four children.

Lodewijk Reinier Jan Anthonie Roosmale Nepveu

The text used is excerpted from two letters by Roosmale Nepveu that were published October 4 and October 11, 1893, "Brieven uit Canada", in *Het Oosten: weekblad gewijd aan Christelijke philanthropie*. Nijmegen. Translated and edited in *100 Years Ago, Dutch Immigration to Manitoba in 1893*, Windsor (Electa Press) 1993, pages 83–93.

Roosmale Nepveu was born in Zeist on July 15, 1825 into the highest class of Netherlands society; his mother was Baroness Elisabeth Jacqueline Taets van Amerongen and his father was Louis Antoine Roosmale Nepveu. He married Baroness Cornelia Hermina Bentinck van Schoonheten. He joined the military and with the rank of Captain, on June 7, 1858 he became the *aide de camp* of Prince Frederik of the Netherlands, the second son of King Willem I. Later, he would serve as *aide de camp* to Queen Regent Emma, mother of Princess Wilhelmina who was to be the future Queen of the Netherlands. Throughout much of his life, Roosmale Nepveu was deeply committed to evangelism in the Netherlands. For example, he was a member of the executive of the Netherlandic Evangelical Protestant Association and served as President of the Dutch Association for Evangelization of the Military in the Dutch East Indies. Roosmale was also one of the founding members of the Committee of Immigration to Canada, which was responsible for the first group emigration of Dutch citizens to Canada in 1893. That same year, he was appointed to represent the Netherlands by the Evangelical Alliance for the purpose of participating in the international conference of the Alliance at the Chicago World's Fair in 1893. His second son, Henri Rudolph, had emigrated to settle near Yorkton (in what is now Saskatchewan) in 1888. He passed away on December 21, 1904 in Doorn.

Duke Bernhard of Saxe-Weimar-Eisenach

The text used is from: Bernhard, Duke of Saxe-Weimar-Eisenach, *Reize Naar en Door-Amerika, 1825 and 1826*. Dordrecht: Blusse En Van Braam, 1829, Pages 210–218, 220–221, 221–225, 192–194.

Duke Bernhard was born in 1792 in Weimar, Germany in courtly surroundings; his family was amongst others related to the British and Russian royal families. Growing up, he received a very broad education through private tutoring, looking toward a military career. In 1815, he joined the Dutch army. His experiences on the battlefield and reputation for being a man of great intellect supported his rise through military ranks. In 1816, he became Chief Commander of the Dutch Army over East Flanders, based in Ghent (Belgium), which was then still part of Holland.

In 1825, King Willem I requested that Duke Bernhard make an inspection tour of North America. He agreed to make the journey together with A.E. Tromp, a Dutch naval engineer. He also travelled through North America in the company of Wilhelm Böttner, a valet working at the court of Duke Bernhard and his wife, Princess Ida of Saxe-Meiningen, whose sister, Duchess Adelaide, married the Duke of Clarence who became King William IV of England.

During his trip from New York to Niagara Falls, Duke Bernhard was accompanied by Gerardus Balthazar Bosch.[143] Bosch was a Minister at the Reformed Church and a School Inspector at Curacao, in the Dutch West Indies. Bosch's travel chronicle only mentions that he visited the Canadian site of Niagara Falls.

After his return from his American trip, Duke Bernhard held other positions in the Dutch army. In 1848, he was appointed Commander-in-Chief of the Dutch East Indies Army, based at the Dutch colony in what is now known as Indonesia. This assignment turned out to be his last. He returned to the Netherlands in 1851, living in The Hague, and later he returned home to Weimar, Germany. He died on July 31, 1862 in Bad Liebenstein, Germany.

Bernard Christiaan Schuijlenburg

The text is from: Bernard C. Schuijlenburg, *Amerika En Canada, Reisaantekeningen*, Nijmegen: P. J. Geurts, 1890, pages 240–243; 256–259; 275–293.

Schuijlenburg was born in 1854 in Axel, in the province of Zeeland, and obtained his higher education at the military medical school in Amsterdam (1871–1875). Afterwards, he left for the Dutch East Indies where he served in the Koninklijk Nederlandsch-Indisch Leger (the Royal Netherlands East Indies Army). While on leave in Holland, he noticed an advertisement in the local paper about an organized trip to the USA and Canada by J. P. Lissone of *Amsterdam*. On May 26, 1888, he left from Rotterdam for America together with two ladies, three men and a guide, aboard the Holland America Line ship, the Amsterdam. He returned in July of 1890 to Batavia to continue serving in the military in the rank of Captain-quartermaster. On April 5, 1893 in Deil, Holland, he married Maria Kolff. In November 1898, Schuijlenburg was promoted to Major-quartermaster, later receiving an honourable discharge on April 1, 1899. Once he finally returned to Holland, he worked as a Lieutenant Colonel in the Department of Pensions of Colonial Affairs. Schuijlenburg died in The Hague on August 1, 1914.

Ernst Sillem

The text used is from: *De reis om de wereld van Ernst Sillem, 1888–1890*, Agnes Sillem, ed., Amsterdam: Van Soeren & Co., 1997, pages 47–55.

Sillem was born in 1864 into a wealthy and influential family. His father was a partner of the bank Hope & Co., a renowned firm known the world over and, amongst other major ventures, was involved in financing the CPR. After Sillem worked for a year at the bank Baring Brothers & Co. in England, his father sent him on a world tour. Upon his return, he joined the higher ranks of Hope & Co. The journey occurred between 1888–1890 taking him to the USA and Canada and then to China, Japan and the Dutch East Indies. Sillem married Augusta Gaymans in 1890. He passed away on December 20, 1919.

Gerrit Verschuur

The text is from: Gerrit Verschuur, *Door Amerika, Reisherinneringen*, Amsterdam: Gebroeders Binger, 1877, pages 200–229.

Verschuur, who made his trip to North America together with his brother Wouter, was born in Amsterdam in 1840. Verschuur dabbled in the assurance business after he had inherited a large legacy from his father, Wouterus Verschuur, an accomplished artist best known for his paintings of horses. Verschuur travelled around the world and wrote books about his endeavours. In 1877, he made the crossing from France to the island of Martinique in the Caribbean, and then onward to the USA and Canada. While in Montreal, he connected with some Canadian world travellers, whom he had already met in Italy. He never married and, in his later years, Verschuur was able to live a comfortable life style on the Cote D'Azur, where he occasionally entertained Dutch writers. He died on September 20, 1906 in Nice, France.

Cornelis Johannes Wijnaendts Francken

The text is from: Cornelis J. Wijnaendts Francken, *Door Amerika, Reisschetsen, Indrukken en Studiën*, Haarlem: H. D. Tjeenk Willink, 1892, pages 159–174.

Wijnaendts Francken was born on November 14, 1863 in Rotterdam, the son of a minister. In 1890, he received his Doctorate in Biology from the University of Utrecht. Soon afterward, he chose to travel to the USA and Canada to see some friends and, as he put it, "to expand his knowledge, insight and experience". During his life, he continued to travel extensively taking intervals to study subjects such as psychology and sociology at the universities of Jena, Zurich, Paris and Berlin. Wijnaendts Francken was a prolific writer having published about forty books and countless articles covering a wide variety of subjects. In 1935, he initiated the C. J. Wijnaendts Francken Foundation Award for essays, literary criticism, biographies, etc., in Dutch prose. He passed away at Leiden on April 10, 1944.

Appendix B
Report by August E. Tromp

August E. Tromp: Biography

August E. Tromp was born on March 12, 1801 in Zierkzee in the province of Zeeland. On March 12, 1827, he married M. A. C. Hartogh Heys and they had 5 children. Tromp started his career as a cadet in ship construction. In 1821, he obtained a position as an engineering student in Rotterdam at the government-run wharf. During the years 1831 to1839, he worked at De Schelde wharf in Vlissingen. He was certified as a professional engineer in 1839.

In 1843, he was promoted to Chief Engineer of shipbuilding for the navy engineer corps, at the government wharf in Amsterdam. After being passed over for further promotion, in 1857 he left the wharf and became the navy's Chief Engineer of General Works until 1867. Tromp died on June 10, 1871 in Hilversum.

The following excerpt is from Tromp's September 9, 1826 report to His Excellency, the Minister of the Navy and Colonies. Only the Canadian aspects in this report have been translated. (For about two months, he accompanied Duke Bernhard of Saxe-Weimar-Eisenach.) The report covers his visits to a number of harbours in England and through part of the United States of America. The North American sections of it discuss canals in the USA, the most important bridges in the USA, West Point

Military Academy and steamships both in the USA and Canada. On April 2, 1828, Tromp received, by royal decree, 1,000 guilders as a bonus for the completion of this report.

Inland Navigation Steamships

Excerpt from a report under Royal Decree of February 23, 1823, No. 115: *A journey to a number of harbours in England and through part of the United States of North America*, September 9, 1826, August E. Tromp, Junior Engineer of the Navy, De Schelde, Vlissingen, National Maritime Museum, Amsterdam

Frontenac

The steamship *Frontenac* has sailed for 9 years on Lake Ontario, and services the community between the city of Kingston and the small village of Newark. It is one of the largest that one sees in North America. It is a vessel of 750 tons, with a deck length of 170 English feet (51 metres) and of which the largest width is 35 English feet (10 metres). One uses this large ship for the purpose of transporting troops, which has to happen quite often. One could have done this with a much smaller vessel, no matter how turbulent Lake Ontario might be. This is clearly shown by the second vessel, *Queenstown*, of which the measurements are much smaller.

The vessel *Frontenac* is very ungainly and heavy but not sturdily built, because the connection is so bad that the middle part sags by the weight of the engine (a shortcoming that many Canadian ships of this size have).

The interior furnishings have also many shortcomings and would be candidate for considerable improvements. The ladies cabin is neatly fitted, but not the accommodation area for the male passengers, which is also the dining room and where one finds small huts with four bunks on the sides. The engine, built by Bolton & Watt, is 55-horsepower strong, and an older type. Its movements are very irregular; it passes the middle point of movements with hefty shocks, and makes about 20 revolutions in every minute.

Since the engine is placed far above the deck, a wooden enclosure was built over that part of the deck and looks much like a small shed. Overall, the vessel has the appearance of a floating hamlet because beside this box, there is another one built in front of the galley. Furthermore, there is a covered seating or walking area at the middle deck, and beside all this are paddle boxes and other modern conveniences. The engine can generate a speed between 5 and 6 knots. The speed increases up to 7 knots when the wind is favourable. One can also use the sails which are made up of rigging of two masts and square sails. That the vessel cannot go faster, I got from experience, since it covered the distance from New York to Kingston, which is 190 English miles, in 17 hours.

Lady Dalhousie

This vessel is named after the wife of the present Governor General of the English possessions in North America, and sails in the St. Lawrence between the city of Kingston and the hamlet of Prescott.

This vessel was again anything but finely furnished, unlike the steamships that I saw in England and like the ones that are already sailing on the national waters. Even though built only four years ago, her appearance looked miserable.

The length of this vessel is 70 English feet, the width 18 English feet. It is 3½ English feet deep and has a flat bottom for the many shallow spots in the river. The engine, 20-horsepower strong, runs irregularly, jolting with 20 revolutions per minute. The shaft of the instrument is located above the deck and the water paddles are completely made from wood. The captain assured me that they sailed at 8 knots, but according to my observations, I am convinced that the speed can be no more then 7 knots, notwithstanding the strong current that one has when sailing down the river.

Lady Sherbrooke

This vessel is the largest that sails on the St. Lawrence and perhaps with respect to inland shipping, the largest of all in North America. Along with many others, it serves the community between Montreal and the Capital of Upper Canada, the much-reinforced Quebec.

In Montreal, one finds a number of steamships built to transport carriages and cattle that sail to Quebec as well as cross over to the village La Prairie, Longeuil, etc. There is also a steam towboat to tow ships from Quebec to Montreal, being very useful when there is a strong current in the river. This vessel rightfully carries the name *Hercules*, since she has a capacity of 120 horsepower and, in this way, surpasses every other North American steamship. I had heard much praise being spoken about this vessel and therefore I was disappointed that shortly before I arrived in Montreal, it had left to tow a lumber vessel, the *Baron Renfrew*, down the river. Upon my arrival in Quebec, it was already gone, further to the Gulf of St. Lawrence. So, I was not only deprived of having the satisfaction to see this steam tugboat, but also remained deprived of viewing that colossus, which exited only for a short time.

The *Lady Sherbrooke* is a vessel of 800 tons, 151 English feet long and 37 feet wide. The ratio of the width to the length is, consequently 1:4. The vessel has an engine of 60 horsepower that makes on average 10 revolutions per minute and whose movements are more regular than many others by means of an enormously large float that has been added to the instrument. She is however old, much too weak, and not able to provide the unwieldy boat a speed of more then 5 knots, without counting the assistance of the stream

It is the most clear, when working against the stream, the poor proportion between the small engine and the size of the vessel because, under exceptional circumstances, the former can barely prevent it from being driven back. In an unpleasant way, I experienced that during the return trip from Quebec to Montreal in the same vessel, because it took more than two hours to make the last half-mile.

Phoenix

The steamboat *Phoenix*, along with another vessel, sails on Lake Champlain from St. Jean to Whitehall. She was the best furnished that I had seen so far, and competed with the best steam vessels and made, as it were, the transition (the border between Canada and the republic is located at Lake Champlain near Isle Aux Nois) from the English to the American vessels.

The length of this vessel is 120 English feet and the width is 42 English feet including the galleries. Because the deck is continuous, a spacious walkway is created. The engine has 46 horsepower and makes, on average, 21 revolutions in a minute, but runs very irregularly and causes such an unpleasant tremble in the vessel that sleeping was denied to many passengers.

The *Phoenix* was the first Canadian vessel on which I saw a pipe for the discharge of superfluous steam. Normally the steam escapes a little way above the deck and neatly wraps the passengers in wet damp. Even the current was often at our disadvantage — we still sailed with a speed of only about 6 or 7 knots.

The interior layout and furnishing was unsurpassable. In the cabin that is intended for the female passengers, one finds ten sleeping places. Next is a large cabin or dining hall for the male passengers, with 28 bunks (2 metres high) on the sides of it. Outside, there is still another forward cabin with 12 sleeping places. All the rooms are neatly and tastefully furnished — yes, the room of the women could even be called beautiful. On the deck are two neat domes. The first masks the stairways of the ladies' cabin and there is even a small corner to store away their belongings. The second masks the stairway of the first dining hall or grand cabin and there one finds the office of the Captain.

On the whole, the carelessness of the ship workers on the steamships is incomprehensible, and it is this cavalier behavior (not the vessels themselves) to which one can attribute most of the accidents that have taken place with steamships.

Endnotes

[1] Joost van den Vondel, 'Inwydinge van 't Stadthuis t'Amsterdam', *De werken van Vondel*. Vol. 5. 1645-1656 (Amsterdam: De Maatschappij voor goede en goedkoope lectuur, 1931).

[2] Heerlien, Maarten. *Van Holland naar Cupidos Koe, Hollandse Newfoundlandhandel in de context van de Internationlae kabeljauwvisserij bij Newfoundland in de zestiende en zeventiende eeuw*. MA Thesis Rijksuniversiteit Groningen, 2005. See also "Adventures in the Sack Trade: London Merchants in the Canada and Newfoundland Trades, 1627-1648", Peter Edward Pope, *The Northern Mariner/Le Marin du nord*, VI, No. 1 (January 1996), 1-19.

[3] *La Gazette de Québec*, June 7, 1810.

[4] *Montreal Herald*, February 6, 1821 and August 20, 1825.

[5] *Algemeen Handelsblad*, February 16, 1838. "Kort Begrip van den Opstand in Kanada".

[6] Noord-Brabander, August 5, 1845. "Een nieuwe verschrikkelijke brand, Junij 28, Québec".

[7] The *Algemeen Handelsblad*, November 16, 1865, reported in the "Latest News" section that "one expects an attack of the Fenians on Canada in the coming winter".

[8] *Het Nieuws van den Dag*, May 26, 1883. "De eerste Minister van Canada, Sir John Macdonald". General Butt Hewson had alleged that Macdonald had committed perjury in prior litigation between them.

[9] For distilled exports to Canada see: Jan. Th. J. Krijff, *Een Aengenaeme Vrientschap, A collection of historical events between the Netherlands and Canada from 1862 to 1914* (Toronto: Abbeyfield Publishers, 2003) p. 84.

[10] NA, BUZA. 3047, f. 24.

[11] More than one million entrance tickets were sold during the Exhibition. See: Montijn, Ileen, *Kermis van koophandel: De Amsterdamsche Wereldtentoonstelling van 1883* (Bussum: Van Holkema & Warendorf, 1983). An extensive and enthusiastic article entitled "Amsterdam Exhibition, Fine Exhibit by the Canadian Pacific Railway" details the contents of the CPR exhibit. In the red, blue, white, and gold stall, located at one end of the British Section, was a "striking map of Canada, which extend[ed] above the whole length of the exhibit. . . . The line of the Canadian Pacific Railway [stood] out very prominently." The stall contained many samples of grain, woods, minerals, and soil. See *Manitoba Daily Free Press*, Winnipeg, Saturday, July 7, 1883.

[12] *Leeuwarder Courant*, November 3, 1883.

[13] *Sir William Van Horne en de Canadian Pacific Spoorweg*, J. L. Pierson (Leiden, N.V. Boekhandel en Drukkerij voorheen E. J. Brill, 1925). Most of these firms were backed by families, such as Boissevain, Pierson and Sillem, of the "new Amsterdam elite". See B. van Vonderen, *Deftig en Ondernemend, Amsterdam 1870-1910* (Amsterdam: Meulenhoff, 2013).

[14] Emma Albani, Dame. She writes in her autobiography that her audience in The Hague and Amsterdam were "most enthusiastic".

See: Emma Albani, *Forty Years of Song*, (London: Mills Boon Limited, 1911).

[15] *Het Nieuws van den Dag*, September 4, 1884.

[16] *Het Nieuws van den Dag*, August 11, 1886, p.1. Division 1. Milling. Class: 1. Raw Produce; Gold Medal for Wheat; Silver Medal for other Grains and Legumes.

[17] *Het Nieuws van den Dag*, February 8, 1866, p. 4.

[18] Gerard Christian Coster was born July 20, 1811, son of Haro Jaochim Coster and Catharina Maria de Reus. On January 28, 1834, Coster purchased the manor 'Vrijenhoeve' near Alphen aan den Rijn. He died on April 27, 1837 in Amsterdam at the house of his brother, J. G. Coster. See Archive of the Family van Dijk van 't Velde (1689–1991) at the Regionaal Archief Zutphen, Zutphen.

[19] Gerard C. Coster to J. Smaale de Reus, February 22, 1831. Archive No. 399, Familie Westerman en aanverwante Families, Gemeentearchief Amsterdam, Amsterdam.

[20] J. L. Pierson, *Sir William Van Horne en de Canadian Pacific Spoorweg* (Leiden: N. V. Boekhandel en Drukkerij voorheen E. J. Brill, 1925).

[21] W. T. Gevers-Deynoot, *Aantekeningen op eene reis door de Verenigde Staten van Noord-Amerika en Canada in 1859* ('s-Gravenhage, 1860).

[22] G. Verschuur, *Door Amerika, Reisherinneringen* (Amsterdam, 1877).

[23] B. C. Schuijlenburg, *Amerika En Canada, Reisaantekeningen* (Nijmegen, 1890).

[24] C. J. Wijnaendts Francken, *Door Amerika, Reisschetsen, Indrukken en Studiën* (Haarlem, 1892).

[25] Bernhard, Duke of Saxe-Weimar-Eisenach, *Reize Naar en Door Noord-Amerika*, 1825–1826 (Dordrecht, 1829).

[26] L. R. Koolemans Beijnen, *de Reis Der Pandora naar de Noordpoolgewesten in den zomer van 1875* (Amsterdam: C. F. Stemler, 1876).

[27] Jan Rudolf Mees, *Dagboek Van Eene Reis Door Amerika* (Rotterdam, 1988).

[28] *Een Amsterdammer in Amerika 1866–1867, Verslag van de reis van Claude August Crommelin* door de Verenigde Staten en Canada, eds., Guus Veenendaal en H. Roger Grant (Amsterdam: De Bataafsche Leeuw, 2009).

[29] *De reis om de wereld van Ernst Sillem 1888–1890*, ed. Agnes Sillem (Amsterdam: Van Soeren & Co., 1997).

[30] K. J. Kuipers, *"Lotgevallen van K. J. Kuipers te Obergum op zijne gedane Zee-en Landreizen den jare 1790 tot en met 1818"* (Groningen, 1844), Jakob Klatter ed. (Zutphen: De Walburg Pers, 1980).

[31] J. C. Gevers to the Minister of Foreign affairs, August 26, 1845, Nationaal Archief, BUZA 1813–1870, Inv. nr. 1381.

[32] C. D. W. Boissevain, "Brieven uit Canada", *Algemeen Handelsblad* (Amsterdam, 1892).

[33] Jaap Moes, *Onder Aristocraten, Over hegemonie, welstand en aanzien van adel, patriciaat en andere notabelen in Nederland, 1848-1914*, (Hilversum: Verloren, 2012), p. 47.

[34] Claudius Frederik Willem Gevers (1830–1907) was a lawyer at the Supreme Court of the Netherlands.

[35] King Willem I, born as Willem Frederik Prince of Orange-Nassau (1772–1843) was King of the Netherlands from 1815–1840.

[36] For the text of the Rush-Bagot Agreement of 1817, see "Treaties affecting Canada in force between His Majesty and the United States of America" (Ottawa: King's Printer, 1927), p.12.

[37] See Appendix B.

[38] It is perhaps poignant to know that the Dutch Government was not vigorous in eradicating this injustice; it was not until July 1863 that slavery was officially abolished in the Dutch colony, Suriname.

[39] Susana Grymes was born as Cayetana Susana Bosque Y Fanqui on August 7, 1796 in New Orleans and died December 3, 1854 in New Orleans. She was first married to Governor William C. C. Claiborne. She remarried John R. Grymes, attorney and legislator on December 1, 1822.

[40] The Lower House is the second chamber of the Estates General, the parliament of the Netherlands.

[41] (Footnote from original text) It will be opened for traffic at the end of 1859.

[42] The Dutch engineer, Thomas J. Stieltjes, tested the specifications used by Robert Stephenson for the construction of the Victoria Bridge, theoretically. J. Stieltjes (1819–1878) as a model in his draft for the projected bridge at the Moerdijk, published in 1860. *De groote Victoriabrug in Canada, en de geprojecteerde brug aan den Moerdijk; of de theorie van T.J. Stieltjes, getoest aan de praktijk van Rob. Stephenson*, (Rotterdam: Nijgh, 1860).

[43] (Footnote from original text) One calculates that the width of the curve of the water where it starts to fall in the midst of the horseshoe is more then 20 feet. One tries to prove this in an odd

way. In 1829, one old ship of 18 feet long was loaded with a living bear, a deer, a buffalo and various small animals and was set free at some distance above the fall. Already before the ship reached the shore, it was partially smashed, but the hull remained intact, and made the jump without hitting the rocks. After the fall there was, of course, nothing to see of it.

[44] The *Asia* is one the ships of the Cunard Line, sailing between Liverpool and New York City.

[45] 'Blondin' is a pseudonym of Jean Francois Gravelet, (b. Feb 28, 1824, St. Omer, France; d. Feb 19, 1897, London). Known to be the most famous of Niagara's daredevils, he was a tightrope walker and acrobat. He owed his fame and fortune to his feat of crossing the Niagara Falls on an 1,100 feet long tight rope, strung 160 feet above the water. He crossed the Niagara Falls several times, either blindfolded, on stilts, trundling or carrying a man on his back.

[46] The Niagara River near the Niagara Falls was one of the numerous places were many of the estimated 40,000 fugitive slaves escaped their misery and found their way to freedom in Canada. Through a network of people known as the 'Underground Railroad', slaves were assisted across the border, for example, by crossing the Niagara River. The Nathaniel Dett Memorial Chapel, British Methodist Episcopal Church, constructed by former slaves in 1836 in Niagara Falls, is one of the many Historic Sites of Canada.

[47] *Het Nieuws van den Dag*, April 6, 1888, "Travel presentation by Mister Lissone, Friday evening 6 April, Odeon Theatre Hall, at the Singel in Amsterdam".

[48] Jac. P. Lissone managed a parcel delivery service between Amsterdam and London. In 1876, he acted successfully as a travel guide on a trip to London after which he set up a travel agency. He was a pioneer in organized packaged tours for tourists going to the USA and Canada. After a merger, Lissone became known as

Lissone-Lindeman, once a household name and, until the 1960s, was also involved with Dutch emigration to Canada. After being acquired by Holland International in 1974, the name disappeared.

[49] Anti-British sentiment in Ireland became a movement after The Great Famine (1845–1848) and also spread across the Atlantic to the USA with Irish immigrants. It was believed that by attacking Canada from the USA, England would loosen its grip on Ireland. Between April and June of 1866, there were a number attempts to invade the British North American colonies, however, without success. The last attack was in 1870 at the border between Manitoba and Minnesota and ended in defeat, thus bringing to an end the Fenian invasions.

[50] The 'Rossin House' counted as one of Toronto's most fashionable hotels. It has its origin in 1864 when a group of Toronto gentlemen made an application for incorporation to establish a hotel under the name 'Rossin House Hotel'. The capital in stock amounted to $96,000, counting 480 shares with a value of $200 (*La Gazette du Canada*, October 22, 1864). Among the applicants were politicians such as: George Brown, David Lewis Macpherson, John Ross; and the financiers: Kazimierz S. Gzowski, George M. Hawke, John Macdonald, Alexander Manning, Marcus Rossin and Benjamin Homer-Dixon. The latter was born in Amsterdam and became the first Dutch Consul-General in Canada.

[51] Schuijlenburg travelled with an engineer, an ex-civil servant of the post office, a retired navy officer and two unmarried ladies from 's-Gravenhage, together with a young guide from London.

[52] The arrival of Duke Bernhard of Saxe-Weimar-Eisenach was reported in the *Kingston Chronicle* of Friday, September 2, 1825: "His Serene Highness who is married to a sister of the Duchess of Clarence was received with a Royal Salute." He was described as being "remarkably courteous and agreeable in his deportment".

[53] Duke Bernhard travelled through Canada in the company of his personal court valet, Wilhelm Böttner, and A. E. Tromp, a navy officer. During the leg from New York to Niagara Falls, he was also accompanied by Gerardus Bosch. See Appendix A.

[54] Robert Flack from Syracuse, New York drowned on July 4, 1888, while attempting to navigate the Whirlpool Rapids in a boat.

[55] John R. and Cayetana Susana Bosque Y Fanqui Grymes. John Grymes (1786–1854) was Attorney General in New Orleans, a member of the Louisiana Legislature and a member of the Louisiana Constitutional Convention.

[56] Sir Michael and Lady Clare. Sir Michael was a member of the Parliament of Jamaica.

[57] The city of Namur is located in the south of Belgium.

[58] Jean-Baptiste Juchereau Duchesnay (Feb. 16, 1779-Jan. 13, 1833). In March 1821, he was named provincial *aide de campe* by Governor Lord Dalhousie. This appointment gave him the rank of Lieutenant Colonel in the militia.

[59] Elias Walker Durnford (July 28, 1774 to March 8, 1850). From 1816 to 1831, he was the Commanding Engineer for Upper and Lower Canada. While stationed in Quebec, he superintended the erection of the citadel in Quebec City and fortifications at Quebec.

[60] Verschuur, *Nieuw Nederlandsch Biografisch Woordenboek*, 1918, Vol. IV, p. 1299.

[61] There are about a dozen Canadian photographs, amongst them are a few by J. G. Parks, Montreal, Wereld Museum, Rotterdam, the Netherlands.

[62] Pio Palazzi, *Commemorazione di Giovanni Tomasoni, Letta Il 14 Giugno 1881 Nella Chiesa Del, B, Pellegrino In Padova, dal Consigliere D'Admnistrazione Della Casa Di Ricovero*, (Padova: Tipografia Alla Minerva Fratelli Salmin, 1881).

[63] Tadoussac is the oldest village in Canada and the site of the first official fur trading post in Canada. The Tadoussac red roof hotel was built in 1866, and still welcomes hundreds of visitors every year.

[64] One German mile is 7407 metres, used in nautical navigation.

[65] The *Prospect* was cleared at Custom-House on June 6th, according to the Quebec Gazette of Tuesday June 28, 1810.

[66] Kuipers made a slight error, here. The time frame was 1759–1810, 58 years.

[67] Kuipers was one of the spectators who witnessed, on June 3, 1811, the placement of a large cross, in the presence of Bishop Joseph-Octave Plessis, representing the first stone laid in the construction of the first Catholic Church of Saint-Roch. Saint-Roch is a suburb of Lower Quebec City that was expanding as a result of the influx of people connected with a growing shipbuilding industry. See: John Hare, *Histoire De La Ville Québec 1608–1871*, (Montreal: Boréal, 1987), p. 168.

[68] Sir Francis Burton, Governor of Lower Canada (1824-1–1825).

[69] The arrival of Duke Bernhard from Quebec in Montreal and the salute he received as he landed at the St. Helen batteries on Thursday afternoon (September 8) was mentioned in the *Montreal Herald* of Saturday, September 10, 1825.

[70] William Bingham Jr. married Marie-Charlotte Chartier de Lotbinière (1805–1866) in 1821. She was a daughter of Marquis

Michel E. G. A. Chartier de Lotbinière of Quebec. Bingham Jr. was the only son of Senator William Bingham (1751–1804), a wealthy Philadelphia citizen with an international reputation, who maintained business relations with the finance house, Barings of London, as well as with the firms Hope & Co. and Willink of Amsterdam.

[71] It is most likely that Duke Bernhard refers to Miss Frances Ermatinger (1804–1884). She was a daughter of Charles Oakes Ermatinger (1776–1833, born in Montreal) and Charlotte Kalawabide (Kattawabide/Cattoonalute/ Manacowe, died in 1858) who was the daughter of Kadowaubeda (Brooken-Tooth or DeBreche), an Ojibwe Chief. Frances was considered to be the most beautiful daughter (of several children) and was about 21 years old at the time she met Duke Bernhard. Contrary to the Duke's comment, it was not Frances' father, but her grandfather, Lawrence Edward Ermatinger (1736–1789), who was born in Switzerland. See: W. Briant Stewart, *The Ermatingers, A 19th-Century Ojibwa-Canadian Family* (Vancouver: UBC Press, 2007).

[72] The Saint Lawrence Hall Hotel was opened in 1851. It was located at 13 Great Saint James Street, Montreal. The owner was Henry Hogan (d. 1902). Prominent guests included the Prince of Wales, Charles Dickens, John A. Macdonald and George Brown.

[73] The Hotel Richelieu was considered the most prestigious French-Canadian hotel during the last decades of the 19th century. It was built in 1858 by Joseph Beliveau in Montreal on the Rue Saint Vincent. The building was demolished in 1912.

[74] Giovanni Tomasoni (1821–1881) was an Italian lawyer and a well-known public figure in the city of Padua, Italy, where a statue erected in his honour still stands. See also: Pio Palazzi, *Commemorazione di Giovanni Tomasoni letta il 14 giugno 1881, Nella Chiesa Del B. Pellegrino In Padova.* (Padova: Tipografia Alla Minerva Fratelli Salmi, 1881).

[75] James Lillie Graham (1873–1975) was a Canadian landscape painter. He spent 13 years in Europe, of which some time was in the Netherlands. He studied at the Art Association of Montreal with Brymner.

[76] William Brymner (1855–1925) was a Scottish-Canadian painter who moved from Paris to Montreal in 1886.

[77] Boissevain is referring to the Arti & Amicitae Society which maintained an exhibition building of art at the Rokin, Amsterdam. Scheltema & Holkema was a book dealer in Amsterdam and Francois Buffa & Sons was an art dealer in Amsterdam.

[78] The Concertgebouw, which opened its doors to the public on April 11, 1888, is the concert hall in Amsterdam and is currently the home of the Royal Concertgebouw Orchestra.

[79] The Paleis van Volksvlijt in Amsterdam was an exhibition building erected in 1864 and was mostly used for the arts and leisure, such as music, ballet, theatre, opera and operetta. The building was destroyed by fire in 1929.

[80] Hendrik Willem Mesdag (1831–1915) was a Dutch marine painter who belonged to the 'Haagsche School' (the Hague School). Anton Mauve was born in 1838, in Zaandam. He was a painter, aquarellist and etcher. He was also a cousin of Vincent van Gogh.

[81] William Sullivan Barnes (1841–1912) was minister of the Church of the Messiah (Unitarian) in Montreal from 1879–1909. He received an honourary LL.D. from McGill University.

[82] Abraham Keuenen (1828–1891) was a Professor of Theology at the University of Leiden; Julius Wellhausen (1844–1918) was a German biblical scholar; and William Robertson Smith (1828–1891) was a Scottish biblical scholar. All were supporters of

modern theology that stated that the Bible was a fusion of several documents edited by priests.

[83] René Robert H. toe Laer, was a C.P.R. agent for continental Europe in Amsterdam. His sister, Ottoline Henriette was married to Athanase Adolphe Henri Boissevain, who, in 1875, started the firm Adolphe Boissevain & Co., that provided financing for the construction of the Canadian Pacific Railway.

[84] William Cornelius Van Horne was the General Manager (1881–1888), President (1888–1899) and Chairman of the Board of the C.P.R. (1899–1911). He died in 1915.

[85] Burson, Rev. Arthur, Presbyterian Minister, was a member of the Toronto Society Blue Book.

[86] Robert Kilgour of 'Kilgour Brothers, Manufacturers and Printers of Wrapping Paper, Pay-bags, Flour Sacks and Paper Boxes, Importers of Twines', 21–23 Willington Street West, Toronto.

[87] Kazimierz S. Gzowski, (later Sir Kazimierz) was a prominent Canadian, who was born in Russia and died in Toronto in 1898. He was a civil engineer and instrumental in organizing the Canadian Society of Civil Engineers.

[88] Aconite is 'monkshood', commonly used as a sedative.

[89] Sillem met Rudolph Vincent Martinsen in New York before his visit to Canada. Martinsen was a partner with the Amsterdam finance firm Adolphe Boissevain & Co. He represented Dutch interests in a syndicate which financed the C.P.R. with a capital of $30 million. He was also a member of the Board of the C.P.R. He was born in 1851 in Reval, Estonia (then part of Germany). He died in 1892 in New York. See also: W. Kay Lamb, *History of the Canadian Pacific Railway*, (New York: Macmillan Publishing Co., Inc. 1977), p. 93.

⁹⁰ Maclaine Watson & Co. was an established merchant and trading house in Batavia, in the Dutch East Indies. The firm was established in 1827 by a Scottish lawyer, Gillian Maclaine.

⁹¹ McLeod, Rev. John, Methodist Minister. Retired in 1911.

⁹² William Hare, 3rd Earl of Listowell, was known as Viscount Ennismore, was born May 29, 1833 and died June 5, 1924. He was, according to *Medical News* (vol. 53, December 1, 1888, p. 628) lying at the point of death in hospital in Victoria with typhoid fever.

⁹³ 'Gudo' is Augusta Gaymans, who was born on November 14, 1870 in Siak on Sumatra, in the Dutch East Indies. She married Ernst Sillem on May 1, 1890 and died in 1946.

⁹⁴ Thomas M. Henderson was a druggist in Victoria, British Columbia.

⁹⁵ William Fitzherbert Bullen was born in 1857 in Ontario and came to Victoria in 1878. He worked as a manager at the Albion Iron Works until 1893. He was married to Annie Amelia Bush, granddaughter of James Douglas, the Governor of British Columbia from 1858 to 1864.

⁹⁶ Godfried Leonard Baron van Boetzelaer was born January 2, 1871 in De Bilt and passed away on June 6, 1951 in Utrecht. On April 27, 1899, he married Maria Alaide Mathilda De Joncheere (1877–1948). Van Boetzelaer accompanied Colenbrander throughout the journey.

⁹⁷ For more on the relationship between van de Merwede Quarles Van Ufford, see the Colenbrander biographical note, Appendix A.

⁹⁸ This ship (4,539 gross tonnes) was built in 1881 by Hartland and Wolff, at Belfast, Ireland. It was originally named the *Asiatic* and later renamed the *Arabic*. It was purchased in 1890 by the

Nederlandsch-Amerikaansche Stoomvaart Maatschappij and renamed *Spaarndam*. In April 1901, it was sold for scrap.

[99] John Knuppe was a former Dutch army officer who was once employed by the St. Paul & Pacific Railway Co. Knuppe was the brother-in-law of Johan Carp, who had bargained in 1877 on behalf of Dutch financiers when the St. Paul & Pacific Railway Co. stopped paying interest on its loan.

[100] Jan Boon Hartsinck was born in 1851 in Deventer. He was, along with Knuppe, a representative of the Netherlands-America Land Company in St. Paul, Minnesota. Previously, he had worked for the CPR and the Qu'Appelle Valley Farming Co. in Saskatchewan.

[101] Henricus 'Henk' Appollonius Johannes Leembruggen was a member of the Committee for Emigration that sent 69 Dutch immigrants to Winnipeg in 1893. See: J. Th. J. Krijff, *100 Years Ago, Dutch Immigration to Manitoba in 1893*, (Windsor: Electa Press, 1993).

[102] Both men stayed at *The Manitoba*, a hotel located at the corner of Main Street and Water Avenue. Built in 1890 for the Northern Pacific and Manitoba railway, the so-called "Grandest Hotel in the West", burnt down on February 18, 1899.

[103] Henri Rudolph Roosmale Nepveu was born October 13, 1862 in 's Gravenhage. Nepveu grew up in an upper-class family and emigrated to Canada in 1888. Henri farmed for many years near Yorkton, Saskatchewan and died July 8, 1947 in Winnipeg, Manitoba. Henri's father Louis R. J. A. Roosmale Nepveu was a member of the Committee of Emigration. See Krijff, *100 Years Ago*, p. 25.

[104] Frederik Robert Insinger was born December 6, 1862 in Brummen. His family belonged the financial establishment in Amsterdam. He emigrated to Canada in 1885 and started

ranching at Willowbrook, Saskatchewan. He was an elected member of the Council of the Legislative Assembly for the North West Territories, for the districts of Wallace (from 1892 to 1894) and Yorkton (from 1894 to 1897). Soon afterward, he moved to Spokane and became the President of the Holland Bank. See also Krijff, *100 Years Ago*, p. 27.

[105] 'Jek' is likely the nickname of Henriette Egbertine, Frederik Colenbrander's sister. She married Mauritz Pico Diederik Baron van Sytzama on Oct 7, 1898, who was mentioned in one of Colenbrander's letters.

[106] Leembruggen was born January 24, 1840 in Hillegom and was raised at his family's country house 'Veenenburg' in Lisse. He later lived on the country estate 'de Bese' in Dalfsen. The family owned the Clos & Leembruggen spinning mills in Leiden since 1766. He married Henrietta Jacoba Dorothea Maria Mispelblom Beijer (born in Zutphen on September 1, 1847) in Zutphen in 1867.

[107] The *Albion Hotel* was operated by its proprietor, Angus Mcleod. This three-storey hotel was built in 1890 and was heated with hot air. It had "forty good bedrooms" according to the *Manitoba Daily Free Press*, May 20, 1890.

[108] Edith Jane Miller, contralto, was born circa 1875 and raised in Portage la Prairie. During her time, she was known as 'The Manitoba Nightingale'. She studied in Toronto, Canada; London, England; and in Paris, France. She moved to England where, in 1911, she sang with Emma Albani at the Crystal Palace. She married Sir Thomas Colyer-Fergusson of Wombwell Hall and died June 1936 in Gravesend, England. Source: *The Montreal Gazette*, July 11, 1936.

[109] 'Reuversweerd' is a large country house built around 1830, located near Brummen, and was famous for its horse-breeding and stables. The house is presently owned by the family of Baron van Zytzama, but is not habitable.

[110] Richard Seeman, of London, England acquired a homestead near Theodore, Saskatchewan in 1892, becoming Theodore's first postmaster in 1893.

[111] De Vries, Heeres and Kamminga were among the group of 68 immigrants arriving in Winnipeg in 1893, arranged by the Committee of Emigratie.

[112] Young Rudolph Baron Bentinck was a cousin of Henri Roosmale Nepveu, his mother being Cornelia Hermina Anna Barones Bentick van Schoonheten. She was born September 24, 1829 in Raalte.

[113] This is probably Jacob Sillevis, born February 2, 1867, in s' Gravenhage. In 1905, he would become the owner of the machine factory De Rijnstreek in Oudshoorn. *De Rijnbode*, nieuws en advertentieblad, Alphen aan de Rijn, May 28, 1937, p. 5.

[114] These immigrant families also came to Canada in 1893, but after the first group of 68 who had come under the Committee of Emigration in April of that year, *supra*.

[115] Klaas de Vries arrived with his brother, Reindert, in 1892. See *Leaving Home Forever, Dutch Pioneers in the Canadian West*, Klaas and Reindert de Vries, Hendrika Ruger ed. preface by J. Th. J. Krijff, (Windsor: Electa Press, 1995).

[116] *Het Lampje* was likely a Christian newsletter.

[117] Henry Hospers was born February 6, 1830 in Hoog Blokland. In 1840, he came to Pella, Iowa, where he would be elected as mayor. There, he established the first newspaper in Dutch. In 1870, he became the leader of a Dutch colony called Orange City. He spent also time as a Republican legislator. He died October 21, 1901 in Orange City. F. Gue Benjamin, *History of Iowa from the Earliest Times to the Beginning of the Twentieth Century*, Vol. 4: "Iowa Biography", Chicago: Century History, 1903.

[118] Baron Joseph John Fagel (1859–1928) attended the University of Utrecht 1881–1885. He was a member of the student society, Tres Faciunt Collegium, which was essentially a club for nobility. He was a member of the board of Noord-Celebes Mijnbouw-Maatschappij, a mining company operating in the Dutch East Indies with the head office in Amsterdam. He was also a member of the Johanniter Order in the Netherlands, membership of which was restricted to Protestant nobility. With his death, the highly esteemed and powerful Fagel family dynasty came to an end.

[119] C. R. van Lelyveld, *Een Arbeid van Vijf-en-Twintig Jaren, in Het Noorden Onzes Lands*, 1884–1909, Der Weesinrichting, Neerbosch 1909.

[120] Roosmale Nepveau is referring to the the Regina Indian Industrial School, one of many which were operated in Canada during the latter part of the 19th century and the early part of the 20th century, to encourage the assimilation of First Nation people. The Regina school operated between 1891 and 1910, burning down in 1948. See *Victorian Ideologies of Gender and the Curriculum of the Regina Indian Industrial School, 1891-1910*, April Rosenau ChiefCalf, M.A Thesis, University of Saskatchewan, Saskatoon, 2002.

[121] Thomas Mayne Daly was born August 16, 1852 in Stratford, Ontario and died June 24, 1911 in Winnipeg, Manitoba. A Liberal Conservative, in 1882 he was the first mayor elected in the city of Brandon, Manitoba and was reelected in 1884. He also served as the first judge of the juvenile court in 1909 in Winnipeg.

[122] (Footnote from original text) A short time ago the population of Montreal amounted to 216,000 residents; Toronto, 181,000 residents; Quebec 63,000 residents; Ottawa 44,000 residents; Winnipeg 25,000 residents; Victoria 16,000 residents; Vancouver 13,000 residents.

[123] (Footnote from original text) One can find an article about this in the *Revue des deux Mondes*, March 15, 1886.

[124] The Bell farm was an 1882 initiative by Major Wm. Bell to start 'corporate farming'. The farm was 53,000 acres and located near Indian Head, Saskatchewan. In 1896, due to the economic climate, the farm was sold and split up into smaller parcels.

[125] During the first half of the 19th century, the Netherlands was generally assumed to be in a sluggish economic situation, which remained until the mid-20th century. Recent historical research shows that this has been a misconception and that the period in question did show some industrial innovation and economic growth. See Joost Jonker: *Merchants, Bankers, Middlemen: The Amsterdam money market during the first half of the 19th century* (NEHA, Amsterdam, 1996).

[126] Jan Salie is a literary character used to symbolize the lack of entrepreneurial spirit in the book *Jan, Jannetje en hun jongste kind* by E. J. Potgieter. The writer aimed to stimulate the sluggish national spirit. See Nederlanders op reis in Amerika 1812-1860, Reisverhalen als bron voor negentiende-eeuwse mentalitieit, Pien Steringa, Utrechtse Historische Cahiers, Jaargang 20 (1999) nr. 1, Universiteit Utrect.

[127] Sir Allen Young, Arctic explorer in search of Sir John Franklin. Born December 12, 1827, Twickenham, Middlesex, England. He made two voyages to the Arctic, one in 1875 and one in 1876. He died in 1915.

[128] William Baffin was an English explorer who died on January 23, 1622.

[129] The *Resolute* and the *Assistance* were part of a four-ship British navy expedition commissioned in 1852 to search for Franklin. The two other ships were *Intrepid* and *Pioneer*. The commander of the expedition was Captain Sir Edward Belcher.

[130] Lancaster Sound is a body of water in Nunavut located between Devon Island and Baffin Island, which makes up the eastern part of the Northwest Passage.

[131] The *Pandora* was a Royal Navy ship built in 1861 at the Pembroke Dock dockyard in South Wales. It was 44.4 metres long and 7.8 metres wide with an 80 horsepower engine that was built by Day Summers & Co., Southampton, England.

[132] Barrow Strait. Shipping waterway in North Canada, Nunavut, part of the Parry Channel.

[133] Sir John Ross was a Scottish Admiral and Arctic explorer, born 1777 and died 1856 in London, England.

[134] Lieutenant Joseph René Bellot (1826–1853) was a French Arctic explorer, who died in 1853 in the Wellington Channel of the Canadian Arctic.

[135] Sir John Franklin was a British Naval officer and Arctic explorer. Born April 16, 1786 in Spilsby, England he died June 11, 1847 on King William Island, Nunavut.

[136] Sir Edward Belcher was a British Naval officer and Arctic explorer born in Halifax, Nova Scotia in 1799, he died 1877. In 1852, he was the commander of an Arctic expedition in search of Sir John Franklin.

[137] (Footnote from original text) Admiral Sherard Osborn, in a lecture held on April 28, 1873 for the Royal Geographical Society, disclosed his belief that the Parry Islands must extend in a westerly direction up to the [Wrangel Laud].

[138] The vessels *Erebus* and *Terror* sailed in 1845 from London under the command of Sir John Franklin in search for the Northwest Passage. The combined crew of 134 men perished in an attempt to reach a safe haven at a Hudson's Bay post in the north.

[139] James Clark Ross was a British explorer and Naval officer (1800–1862). Ross was part of Arctic expeditions with Sir William E. Perry from 1819–1827.

[140] Boothia Peninsula (formerly Boothia Felix) is a large peninsula south of Somerset Island, Nunavut. The Peninsula was named after Felix Booth, the patron of John Ross' second polar expedition in 1829.

[141] Francis Leopold M'Clintock (1819–1907) was born in Ireland and became an Arctic explorer in the British Navy. In 1857 he commanded the ship *Fox* (177 tonnes) in an expedition to attempt to recover any survivors of the Franklin expedition.

[142] Cape Grinnell was named after Henry Grinnell (1799–1874), a wealthy American merchant who financed two exploring expeditions, in 1850 and 1853, in search of John Franklin.

[143] Gerardus Balthazar Bosch was a clergyman at the Verenigde Protestansche Gemeente in Curacao. He travelled with Duke Bernhard from New York to Niagara Falls. See: G. B. Bosch, "Eene Zomerreis in Noord-Amerika", *Vaderlandsche Letteroefeningen*, 1827.

Image Credits

Front cover: *Algerian*, William Henry Jackson, Library of Congress, Prints and Photographs Division, Detroit Publishing Company Collection

Back cover: Winnipeg CPR Station, 1897

Page	Description
xix	Advertisement re: Emma Albani's first appearance in the Netherlands, *Het Nieuws van den Dag*, February 4, 1881
xix	Dame Emma Albani, Canadian opera singer, 1874, cover image, journal Paris *Théâtre-Hebdo*, author's collection
xxxi	Map 1 showing route taken by most of the earliest Dutch travellers, T. Bal, Qualicum Beach, British Columbia
2	Halifax from Dartmouth 1842, drawn by W. H. Bartlett. The front of the town with ships, warehouses and wharfs, amongst which is the Cunard wharf. Nova Scotia Archives and Records Management, Image 201001222.tif
5	*Burlington* steamboat drawing, author's collection
7	W. T. Gevers-Deynoot, Foto Iconografisch Bureau/RKD, 's-Gravenhage, the Netherlands.
7	C. F. W. Gevers, Courtesy, Baron F. A. Gevers, Geneva, Switzerland
10	Donegana Hotel, Notre Dame Street, Montreal, William Notman about 1860. McCord Museum of Canadian History, Notman Photographic Archives View-7463.1

12   Centre tube, Victoria Bridge, Montreal, Quebec, 1869, William Notman, McCord Museum of Canadian History, Notman Photographic Archives, N-0000.193.135

17   Military College Kingston, Ont., about 1890. Wm. Notman & Son, McCord Museum of Canadian History, Notman Photographic Archives. View-2272.1

22   Table Rock Museum and Clifton House 1859, William Notman, about 1860. McCord Museum of Canadian History, Notman Photographic Archives N-0000.193.206.2

25   *Maid of the Mist* 1859. Reproduction: *Maid of the Mist* and American Falls, Niagara, "Copyrighted by M. E. Wright". "Excelsior Stereoscopic Tours, M. E. Wright. Publisher" "Hollingrave Road, Burnley

30   Suspension bridge, Niagara Falls, Ont., William Notman, about 1860. McCord Museum of Canadian History, Notman Photographic Archives N-0000.193.224.2

33   B. C. Schuijlenburg, Courtesy, Mrs. T. van Dam-Schuijlenburg, Rhenen, the Netherlands

34   Lissone advertisement for trip to America and Canada in May. *Het Nieuws van den Dag*, April 5, 1888

37   King and York Streets, looking east on King Street (Toronto, Canada). The Rossin House Hotel is flying the large flag. Date: 1885–1895. City of Toronto Archives, Fonds 1478, Item 22

39   *Spartan* leaving Alexander Bay, Ont., *circa* 1890. McCord Museum of Canadian History, Notman Photographic Archives, View-2277.0.3

41   Duke Saxe-Weimar-Eisenach. Iconografisch Bureau/RKD, 's-Gravenhage, the Netherlands.

50   Congregation of Notre Dame, Nun's Island, William Notman *circa* 1900. McCord Museum of Canadian History, Notman Photographic Archives MP-0000.39.9

52   St. Lawrence Hall, St. James Street, Montreal, QC, *circa* 1890, Wm. Notman & Son, McCord Museum of Canadian History, Notman Photographic Archives, View-1876

61   Interior of Grey Nunnery Chapel, Montreal about 1890, Wm. Notman & Son, McCord Museum of Canadian

History, Notman Photographic Archives, View-2527

64 Montreal harbour near Custom House. William Notman 1865–1875. McCord Museum of Canadian History, Notman Photographic Archives MP-0000.1452.51

66 Dominion Square and Y.M.C.A. building, Montreal. William Notman about 1880. McCord Museum of Canadian History, Notman Photographic Archives, View-2549.1

69 Namur, Belgium, the Meuse River, the Walloon Parliament and the citadel. Photographer, Jean-Pol Grandmont, 2005

70 Colonel Elias Durnford, painting, copied 1861. McCord Museum of Canadian History, I-1718-1

71 Montmorency Falls, Quebec, William Notman 1865. McCord Museum of Canadian History, Notman Photographic Archives, I-17308

73 Joseph-Octave Plessis, Bishop of Quebec, Bibliothèque et Archives Nationales du Québec

76 Quebec, Typical Calèche, author's collection

79 G. Verschuur, Photo 904308, Courtesy, Collectie Wereldmuseum, Nederlands Fotomuseum, Rotterdam, the Netherlands

81 *Saquenay*, reproduction out of, The Lower St. Lawrence River, Ivan S. Brookes, freshwater Press. Inc. Cleveland, Ohio, 1974

85 Timber base at Montmorency, just below Quebec in the 1810s with a distant view of Quebec both Lower and Upper Town. Daniel Wadsworth, National Archives of Canada, C-55617

91 Charlotte de Lotbinière, wife of William Bingham, P6/G4, Fonds Henry de Lotbinière-Harwood, Centre d'histoire La Presqu'ile

93 J. C. Gevers, Courtesy, Baron F. A. Gevers, Geneva, Switzerland

95 Lord Charles T. Metcalfe, 1844, Governor General of Canada, Library and Archives Canada

96 C. A. Crommelin, Courtesy, Liesbeth Crommelin, Amsterdam, the Netherlands

97   Victoria Bridge, Montreal, QC, about 1870, Alexander Henderson, McCord Museum of Canadian History, MP-0000.1452.54

98   Richelieu Hotel, St. Vincent Street, Montreal, Denis Tremblay, 1998. www.old.montreal.qc.ca

99   Giovanni Tomasoni, Courtesy, Museo Civico, Padova, Italy

101   Karel D. W. Boissevain, Courstesy, Mme. I. de Uthemann, Mies, Switzerland

104   Exhibition room, Art Gallery Montreal, QC, 1879, Notman & Sandman, 1879, McCord Museum of Canadian History, Notman Photographic Archives, View-1053.1

108   Former residence of Karel D. W. Boissevain, 434 Metcalfe Ave., Westmount, Montreal, 1993, photographer, Karen B. Green, Heemstede, the Netherlands

112   René R. H. toe Laer, Courtesy, Mrs. D. de Kock-Calkoen, Bilthoven, the Netherlands

113   Ernst Sillem, Courtesy, Agnes Sillem, Lochem, the Netherlands

115   CPR Elevator, Fort William, ON. 1887, William McFarlane, McCord Museum of Canadian History, Notman Photographic Archives, View-1607

116   Winnipeg CPR Station 1897, Archives of Manitoba, Winnipeg "Arrival of harvest excursionists" N22107

119   Vancouver Harbour (1888–1892), Glenbow Archives, Calgary NA 4958-3

121   Esquimalt Harbour Victoria, BC about 1900, author's collection, Postcard, Victoria Book & Stationery

123   Frederik Christiaan Colenbrander, Regionaal Archief Zutphen, Oud Archief Zutphen (arch. Nr. 210), Inv. Nr. 213.

124   Envelope cover from the Manitoba Hotel, Winnipeg, July 24, 1893, author's collection

127   Albion Hotel, Portage la Prairie, from *A History of Portage la Prairie and Surrounding District*, Anne M. Collier, Altona, Manitoba, D. W. Friesen & Sons Ltd. 1970

130 Yorkton, 1896, City Archives of Yorkton, Saskatchewan

135 Lodewijk R. J. A. Roosmale Nepveu, from Kanon, de Bijbelcolporteur, C. R. van Lelyveld, Nijmegen, P. J. Milborn, *circa* 1901

137 Indian Industrial School Regina, 1896-1897, Saskatchewan Archive Board, Regina R-A-1878

138 C. J. Wijnaendts Francken, Morks Magazine, October 1940, Dordrecht, the Netherlands

142 Eau Claire Mill extreme right, Calgary, Alberta, circa 1890, Mather, T. H., Glenbow Archives, Calgary NA 1905-17

143 Major William R. Bell's farm House, Indian Head, Saskatchewan 1884. William McFarlane Notman, McCord Museum of Canadian History, Notman Photographic Archives, View-1386

148 Canadian Pacific Railway bridge across Columbia River at Revelstoke, British Columbia dated 1888–1892, Glenbow Archives, Calgary NA 4958-2

149 Canadian Pacific Railway passenger train with engine 313, Kicking Horse bridge, Alberta, 1896, Glenbow Archives, Calgary NA -967-18

150 Glacier House, British Columbia from the SE (ca. 1887–1889), Boorne and May, Calgary, Alberta, Glenbow Archives, Calgary NA 1798-4

152 Advertisement, Canadian Pacific Railways, *Het Nieuws van den Dag*, April 22, 1899

153 L. R. Koolemans Beijnen, Inv. S.2956 (06), Het Scheepvart-museum, the National Maritime Museum, Amsterdam, the Netherlands

155 Map 2 Route of the *Pandora*, 1875, adapted by T. Bal from map in *Reis der Pandora*, 1876

162 *H.M.S. Pandora*, Inv. S.2956 (04) 22, Het Scheepvart-museum, the National Maritime Museum, Amsterdam, the Netherlands

Bibliography

Manuscript Sources

Gemeentearchief Amsterdam, Amsterdam
Ministerie van Buitenlandse Zaken 1813–1870 Inv. nr. 1381
Nationaal Archief, 's-Gravenhage (N.A.)
National Maritime Museum, Amsterdam
Regionaal Archief Zutphen

Newspapers and Periodicals

Algemeen Handelsblad
De Rijnbode
Het Nieuws van den Dag
Kingston Chronicle
La Gazette de Québec
Leeuwarder Courant
Manitoba Daily Free Press
Montreal Herald
Noord-Brabander
Opregte Haarlemsche Courant
The Montreal Gazette

Selected Bibliography of Dutch Travellers' Writings

Bernhard, Duke of Saxe-Weimar-Eisenach. *Reize Naar en Door Noord-Amerika, 1825–1826*, Dordrecht: Blusse En Van Braam, 1829.

Boissevain, Karel D. W. "Brieven uit Canada." *Algemeen Handelsblad*, 26 April, 15 May 1892.

Letters from Colenbrander, Frederik Christiaan: Regionaal Archief Zutphen, Nr. 210, Familie Colenbrander en de erven van Sytzama 1720–1985, Inv. Nr. 130 Brieven ingekomen van reis door USA en Canada.

De reis om de wereld van Ernst Sillem 1888–1890, Agnes Sillem, ed. Amsterdam: Van Soeren & Co, 1997.

Een Amsterdammer in Amerika 1866–1867, Verslag van de reis van Claude Augustin Crommelin door de Verenigde Staten en Canada, Guus Veenendaal en H. Roger Grant, ed. Amsterdam: De Bataafsche Leeuw, 2009.

Gevers-Deynoot, W. T. *Aaantekeningen op eene reis door de Verenigde Staten Van Noord Amerika En Canada, in 1859*, 's Gravenhage: Martinus Nijhoff, 1880.

Letter from Johan C. Gevers to the Minister of Foreign Affairs, August 25, 1845, Nationaal Archief, Den Haag.

Koolemans Beijnen, L.R. *De Reis Der Pandora, naar de Noordpoolgewsten in de zomer van 1875*, Amsterdam: C. F. Stemler, 1876.

Kuipers, K. J. *Een Groninger Zeeman in Napoleontische Tijd, Zee en Landreizen van K. J. Kuipers, Kleine Handelsvaart Contra Continentaal Stelsel*, J. Klatter, ed. Zutphen: De Walburg Pers, 1980.

Mees, Jan Rudolf. *Dagboek Van Eene Reis Door Amerika 1843–1844*, B. Schoenmaker, ed. Rotterdam: Stichting Historische Publicaties Roterodamun, 1988.

Letters from L. R. J. A. Roosmale Nepveu, excerpt from *Het Oosten: weekblad gewijd aan Christelijk philanthropie*, Nijmegen, 1893. See *100 Years Ago, Dutch Immigration to Manitoba in 1893, pages 83–93*, Krijff, J. Th. J., Windsor: Electa Press 1993.

Schuijlenburg, B. C. *Amerika en Canada, Reisaantekeningen*, Nijmegen: P.A. Geurts, 1890.

Verschuur, G. *Door Amerika, Reisherinneringen*, Amsterdam: Gebroeders Binger, 1877.

Wijnaendts Francken, C. J. *Door Amerika, Reisschetsen, Indrukken en Studien*, Haarlem: H.D. Tjeenk Willink, 1892.

Other Published Sources

Albani, Emma. *Forty Years of Songs*, London: Mills Boon Limited, 1911.

Bosch, Gerardus Baltazhar. *Eene Zomerreis in Noord-Amerika.* Vaderlandsche Letteroefeningen, 1827.

Bosher, J. F. *Men and Ships in the Canada Trade, 1660-1760, A Biographical Dictionary*, Ottawa: National Historic Sites, Park Services, Environment Canada, 1992.

Gue, Benjamin F., *History of Iowa From the earliest Times to the Beginning of the Twentieth Century*, Vol.: 4: Iowa Biography. Chicago: Century History, 1903.

Heerlien, Maarten. *Van Holland naar Cupidos Koe, Hollandse Newfoundlandhandel in de context van de Internationlae kabeljauwvisserij bij Newfoundland in de zestiende en zeventiende eeuw*, MA Thesis, Rijksuniversiteit, Groningen, 2005.

Krijff, J. Th. J. *100 years Ago, Dutch immigration to Manitoba in 1893*. Windsor: Electa Press, 1993.

Krijff, J. Th. J. *Een Aengenaeme Vrientschap*, (An Amicable friendship), *A collection of historical events between the Netherlands and Canada from 1862 to 1914*, Toronto: Abbeyfield Publishers, 2003.

Lelyveld van, C. R. *Een Arbeid van Vijf-en-Twintig Jaren, in Het Noorden Onzes Lands, 1884–1909*, Neerbosch: Weesinrichting, 1909.

Moes, Jaap. *Onder Aristocraten, Over hegemonie, welstand en aanzien van adel, patriciaat en andere notabelen in Nederland, 1848-1914*, Hilversum: Verloren, 2012.

Pierson, J. L. *Sir William Van Horne en de Canadian Pacific Spoorweg*, Leiden: N.V. Boekhandel en Drukkerij voorheen E. J. Brill, 1925.

Rosenau ChiefCalf, April. *Victorian Ideologies of Gender and the Curriculum of the Regina Indian Industrial School*, 1891-1910, M.A Thesis, University of Saskatchewan, Saskatoon, 2002.

Steringa, Pien. *Nederlanders op reis in Amerika, Reisverhalen als bron voor negentiende-eeuwse mentalitieit*, Utrechtse Historische Cahiers, jaargang 20 (1999) nr. 1, Universiteit Utrecht.

Stieltjes, Thomas J. *De Groote Victoriabrug in Canada en de geprojecteerde brug aan den Moerdijk: of de theorie van T. J. Stieltjes, getoetst aan de praktijk van Rob Stephenson*, Rotterdam: Nijgh, 1860.

Vonderen van, Barbara. *Deftig en Ondernemend, Amsterdam 1870-1910*, Amsterdam: Meulenhoff, 2013

Index

Jan Krijff was born in the Netherlands in 1947 and immigrated to Calgary in 1968. After obtaining his B.A. in Economics, he graduated from the University of Leiden with a Masters degree in History. In 1993, Jan published *100 Years Ago, Dutch Immigration to Manitoba in 1893* and in 2003, *Een Aengenaeme Vrientschap (An Amicable Friendship). Greetings from Canada: Postcards from Dutch Immigrants to the Netherlands 1884–1915* was published by Granville Island Publishing in the spring of 2013. He currently lives in the Netherlands with his wife, Karen Green.

Herman Ganzevoort is Emeritus Professor of History, University of Calgary. His publications include *Letters of Willem de Gelder 1910-13: A Dutch homesteader on the prairies; Dutch Immigration to North America; A Bittersweet Land, The Dutch Experience in Canada, 1890-1980; The Last Illusion, Letters from Dutch immigrants in the "Land of opportunity" 1924-1930.* He lives in Calgary with his wife Karen Lynn Fry.